The Judicial Committee of the Privy Council and the Caribbean Court of Justice

The Judicial Committee of the Privy Council and the Caribbean Court of Justice

Navigating Independence and Changing Political Environments

Harold A. Young

LEXINGTON BOOKS
Lanham • Boulder • New York • London

Published by Lexington Books
An imprint of The Rowman & Littlefield Publishing Group, Inc.
4501 Forbes Boulevard, Suite 200, Lanham, Maryland 20706
www.rowman.com

6 Tinworth Street, London SE11 5AL, United Kingdom

British Library Cataloguing in Publication Information Available

Library of Congress Cataloging-in-Publication Data

Names: Young, Harold A., 1962- author.
Title: The Judicial Committee of the Privy Council and the Caribbean Court of Justice : navigating independence and changing political environments / Harold A. Young.
Description: Lanham : Lexington Books, 2020. | Includes bibliographical references and index.
Identifiers: LCCN 2020005552 (print) | LCCN 2020005553 (ebook) | ISBN 9781498586948 (cloth) | ISBN 9781498586955 (epub)
Subjects: LCSH: Courts of last resort—West Indies, British. | Caribbean Court of Justice. | Great Britain. Privy Council. Judicial Committee.
Classification: LCC KGL5501 .Y58 2020 (print) | LCC KGL5501 (ebook) | DDC 347.729/035—dc23
LC record available at https://lccn.loc.gov/2020005552
LC ebook record available at https://lccn.loc.gov/2020005553

Dedicated to my devoted parents, Lester Harold Young and Ernestine Celia Ferreira Young, without whom nothing would be possible.

Contents

List of Figures and Tables

FIGURES

TABLES

Acknowledgments

I thank Dr. Amy Steigerwalt, at Georgia State University, Karla Heusner at the University of Belize, Dr. Nicole Wood at Austin Peay State University and the editors at Lexington Books for their comments on earlier versions of the manuscript. My discussions with many other people greatly helped to improve earlier versions of this manuscript. Any errors are my own and should not tarnish the reputations of these esteemed persons.

Introduction

The comparative study of institutions changes after World War II has accelerated over the decades. Rather than merely comparing structural differences, political scientists start examining how the judiciary performs in terms of effectiveness, independence, and policy preferences. This book provides a window into an intersection of judicial structures and politics. It straddles judicial structures, the role of courts in policy-making, and states' political environments. The goal is to better understand why independent states accede to extraterritorial courts. The term "extraterritorial court" is used to refer to an appellate court exercising appellate jurisdiction, but which can also include original jurisdiction. It has appellate jurisdiction in cases (civil or criminal) originating in any member state involving individuals or legal entities. The work seeks to better understand extraterritorial courts whose adjudicative power, though created by treaty, is not subject to veto by member states. It examines the Judicial Committee of the Privy Council (JCPC),[1] an ancient colonial court, and traces how the Caribbean Community (CARICOM) is transitioning away from the JCPC to its own extraterritorial court, the Caribbean Court of Justice (CCJ)[2] in changing political environments. More specifically, it focuses on the fifteen former British colonies located in and the touching the Caribbean Sea. This is an opportune time to look at this transition period in CARICOM[3] as the CCJ establishes itself and builds credibility. Further, it examines the status of the court as the member states navigate their respective political environments in the deciding whether to remain with the JCPC or replace it with the CCJ. Undoubtedly, this is the first foray into meta-analysis of this type focusing on the Caribbean Basin. It does not purport to answer all questions but to start the analysis of what is an interesting and unique corner of the world of judicial development.

The phenomenon of retaining the JCPC after independence is observed in many former British colonies. Just after midnight on August 15, 1947, the last few bars of "God Save the King" faded into the night. The Union Jack was replaced by "Tiranga," the national flag of India (Mapsofindia 2015), marking the official end of British colonial rule in India. The magnitude of the prowess of British colonial expansion can be captured by one astonishing fact: the day before independence, the United Kingdom, with a population of only 49.5 million people (Populstat 2006a) had controlled the "crown jewel" of the British Empire with its staggering population of almost 400 million (Populstat 2006b) for almost 100 years. In his inaugural address, Prime Minister Jawaharlal Nehru states, "It is a fateful moment for us in India, for all of Asia and for the world. A new star rises, the star of freedom in the East. A new hope comes into being, a vision long cherished materialized" (Prasad 2011). Similar words were heard on every continent.

Part of that vision, however, meant the retention of some aspects of British colonial legal institutions. India's new constitution provided that the Judicial Committee of the Privy Council (JCPC) continue as the final appellate court. Retaining the court was India's own decision, yet within two years, India had replaced the JCPC with the Supreme Court of India as the final appellate court (Jain 2014). India's choice to retain the JCPC court, if only for a little while, was not unique. As the British colonies and territories in Africa, Asia, the Americas, Europe, the Pacific, and Middle East achieved their independence, thirty-two of the sixty-two colonies (52%) retained the JCPC. Currently, eleven states still retain the JCPC, with the most recent to replace it being Dominica in 2016. Even among those states which eventually replaced it with another final appellate court, many countries kept the JCPC for long periods after independence; for example, Australia—1931 to 1986, Malaysia—1958 to 1988, Singapore—1964 to 1987, and New Zealand—1931 to 2005. In addition, there are fourteen overseas territories and colonies that still retain the jurisdiction of the JCPC (The Commonwealth 2015), and eleven former colonies still appeal to the JCPC.

It examines the fascinating intersection of judicial structures and politics, and the role of courts in policy-making and individual states' political environments. Extraterritorial courts whose adjudicative power, although created by treaty, are not subject to veto by member states. More specifically, this study examines the JCPC, an ancient colonial court, and how the CARICOM is transitioning away from the JCPC to its own extraterritorial court, the CCJ in changing political environments. This is an opportune time to look at this transition period in CARICOM as the CCJ establishes itself and builds credibility. At this juncture we can examine the status of the court as the member states navigate their respective political environments to decide whether to remain with the JCPC or replace it with the CCJ. Finally, twelve years data available underpins the analysis of the outcomes of the CCJ with those of the JCPC during the same period (2005–2017).

The development of shared high courts (extraterritorial courts) like the CCJ and the JCPC should not be mistaken for international tribunals or courts such as the International Court of Justice that only adjudicate matters between states. The have appellate jurisdiction in cases (civil or criminal) originating in any member state involving individuals or legal entities. Leave to appeal may be granted by the lower appellate court or by special leave from the JCPC. The former exercise appellate jurisdiction, whereas international tribunals are treaty-based courts of original jurisdiction adjudicating conflicts between states. The development of shared appellate courts by independent nations in the Caribbean is not a new idea.

The European Court of Human Rights (ECtHR), the defunct East African Court of Appeal (EACA), and the CCJ provide templates of developing regional judicial institutions in broader efforts at integration. Extraterritorial courts are part of the ongoing interest in regional and global efforts to foster law and order by adjudicating disputes and responding to challenges to policies set by nation-states. The relationship between extraterritorial courts and states is of great importance because these courts challenge traditional ideas of state sovereignty and the role of courts in the policy-making process. Traditionally, states have created a domestic judicial system with a state high court sitting at the apex. These courts are usually constitutionally authorized, and their structure and processes (including the selection of judges and budgetary matters) are determined by a combination of national constitutional and statutory laws. Most importantly, the decisions of these courts provide the final word for legal disputes within the country's borders. Conversely, extraterritorial courts are located outside state borders, yet they exercise jurisdiction over cases originating in the states that accede to the court. In other words, the extraterritorial court can have jurisdiction in multiple states but is not under the direct administrative control of any single state.

While the constitution and administration of final appellate courts in other jurisdictions are not monolithic, there is a reasonable comparison to be made with the role played by the U.S. Supreme Court in policy-making and that in other states. States can decide on the appointment mechanism, number, and terms of service of the judges, as well as the jurisdiction and funding for domestic courts. Further, most common-law jurisdictions include the power of judicial review comparable to that of the U.S. Supreme Court (Andrade 2001; Tushnet 2004). Not all states, however, have a domestic final appellate court over which they retain administrative control. There are some states with constitutional ties to an extraterritorial judicial entity which then serves as the court of last resort. Not all extraterritorial courts, however, are the same. On the one hand, member states exert a significant degree of control on the European Court of Justice (ECJ) (Alter 1998). Further, the ECJ is part of the growth of European law which is central to the broader process of European integration (Garrett, Kelemen, and Schulz 1998). The World Trade Organization (WTO) also has a judicial function to hear disputes among member nations (World Trade Organization 2015), and the International Court of Justice (ICJ) adjudicates issues that supersede states' domestic jurisdiction making decisions in accordance with international law (International Court of Justice n.d.). Finally, the Inter-American Commission on Human Rights (ICAHR) is an institution of the Organization of American States (OAS) that adjudicates individual claims of human rights violations in states which have signed the American Convention on Human Rights (Organization of American States 2011).

Another example is the African Court on Human and People's Rights (ACHPR). In 2009, the African Union expanded the jurisdiction of the ACHPR to include the international crimes of genocide, war crimes, crimes against humanity, and transnational crimes such as terrorism, piracy, and corruption. Of the fifty-three members of the African Union, twenty-six states have ratified the new protocol (African Court on Human and People's Rights n.d. a). To date, the ACHPR has adjudicated twenty-four cases with thirty pending (African Court on Human and People's Rights n.d. b). Some observers suggest that this new protocol was a step toward undermining the International Criminal Court (du Plessis, Maluwa, and O'Reilly 2013) because the court gave African states more control over the extraterritorial court in general and over the cases that were referred to it for adjudication:

> According to the Protocol (Article 5) and the Rules (Rule 33), the Court may receive complaints and/or applications submitted to it either by the African Commission of Human and Peoples' Rights or State parties to the Protocol or African Intergovernmental Organizations. Non-Governmental Organizations with observer status before the African Commission on Human and Peoples' Rights and individuals from States which have made a Declaration accepting the jurisdiction of the Court can also institute cases directly before the Court. (African Union n.d., para. 4)

The jurisdiction of the ACHPR is limited compared the CCJ. Nevertheless, this is an interesting development because there is not a complete disavowal of extraterritorial courts but instead the replacement of one extraterritorial court for another. This shift may indicate that some states are not generally opposed to extraterritorial courts but are sensitive to the perceived bias of the courts and how their governing policies are constrained by those courts.

The European Court of Human Rights (ECtHR) is another exemplary extraterritorial court. The ECtHR is part of the ongoing process of European integration under the banner of the European Union (EU). Established in 1959, this court has adjudicated 10,000 cases from individuals and states for alleged violations of the European Convention on Human Rights (Council of Europe 2014). One state that has expressed misgivings about continued membership of the ECtHR is the United Kingdom. In 1998, the U.K. Parliament, then dominated by the governing Labour Party, ratified the European Convention on Human Rights. On the other hand, the manifesto of the Conservative Party had pledged to sever ties with the ECtHR and make the U.K. Supreme Court of Judicature the final appellate court in all human rights cases (Travis 2015). Prime Minister Cameron was cited by Watt (June 3, 2015) for refusing to back away from the pledge to withdraw the U.K. from the ECtHR. But Cameron claims that the court's decisions impinge on British sovereignty (Watt June 3, 2015). Further, he refused to rule out abandoning the European Convention on Human Rights unless the U.K. could win the right to veto decisions of the ECtHR. In addressing the U.K. Parliament, the prime minister stated,

> Let me be very clear about what we want, which is British judges making decisions in British courts. . . . If we can't achieve what we need—and I'm very clear about that when we've got these foreign criminals committing offence after offence and we can't send them home because of their right to a family life—that needs to change. And I rule out absolutely nothing in getting that done. (Watt 2015, para. 7)

However, when questioned directly by Andrew Mitchell, another Member of Parliament from the Conservative Party, Prime Minister Cameron stated that there are no immediate plans to abandon the ECtHR (Watt June 3, 2015).

This contention followed a series of decisions by the ECtHR that denied the U.K. the right to deport suspected terrorists (Travis and Watt January 17, 2012; Pearson 2015). The political environment in 2015 with the Conservative Party in power is quite different from that under the Labour Party when parliament ratified the Human Rights Convention in 1998. Further, the unfavorable decisions of the ECtHR came at a time when the governing Conservative Party had publicly expressed its policy objective of limiting the jurisdiction of the ECtHR in the U.K. Nevertheless, no action has been taken because there is discord in the governing coalition. For example, a Conservative member of the House of Lords, Lord Mackay of Clashfern,[4] who served under previous conservative Prime Ministers Thatcher and Major, states that this course of action would send the wrong signal to Europe (Bowcott 2015). There was also discord in other elite circles. Scottish first minister Nicola Sturgeon said any move to scrap the Human Rights Act of 1998 (HRA) will be resisted in Scotland (Simpson 2015). Lord Mance, a judge on the U.K. Supreme Court of Judicature, defended the contributions of the ECtHR to British law while other judges decried the ECtHR as undermining democracy in the U.K. (Henley 2013). Incidentally, Lord Mance was also a Law Lord of the JCPC.

It is evident, therefore, that while the Conservative Party traditionally loathes the ECtHR (Henley 2013), the decisions of the court and political environment have not served to coalesce the political will of the governing coalition to change the status quo. It may also speak to the persistence of the institution once in place and, like the ECJ, its role in the integration of the EU (Garrett, Keleman, and Schultz 1998).

The implications of a possible U.K. withdrawal from the ECtHR is not lost on observers outside of the U.K. Prince Zeid Ra'ad Al Hussein of Jordan, the U.N.'s High Commissioner for Human Rights, states that a U.K. withdrawal would be "profoundly regrettable" (Bowcott 2015, para. 2). A former prosecutor with the International Criminal Count (ICC) and South African Judge, Richard Goldstone, states that it would be a disappointing precedent for the U.K. to set. He concedes that "it would enable some autocratic set of leaders around the world to say, why should we be bound by international law if this great font of democracy, the United Kingdom, is pulling out?" (Elgot 2015, para. 13). It is worth noting that while the conflict provides a window to the tensions between states and extraterritorial courts, the 2016 vote by the U.K. to exit the EU will make the tension moot.

These are just two examples of the tensions that currently exist between states and extraterritorial courts. For states with extraterritorial courts, the domestic appellate courts are the last step in the judicial hierarchical structure before a possible challenge before the exterritorial court over which the governing coalition has no administrative leverage. Because it plays an important role in adjudicating challenges to state policies, the decision to accede to an extraterritorial court would seem to be an affront to state sovereignty and a potential constraint on state policy-making. Why then do states accede to such courts, and what may lead states to later sever ties with them?

To answer these important questions, I begin with the assumption that judges, as well as courts, must be understood as part of the political and judicial decision-making process; Shapiro (1964) refers to this notion as "political jurisprudence." A central issue for all states, therefore, is the organization of the judiciary and the role it plays in policy-making and furthering the "peace, order and good government" (POGG) as a feature of constitutional rule (Yusuf 2014) and state sovereignty. As challenges to policies deemed necessary for POGG percolate up the judicial hierarchy, legitimization of those policies by the judiciary is an important issue (Dahl 1957). Slaughter (2000) and Garrett, Kelemen, and Schulz (1998) point to the interactions of national courts with extraterritorial courts. This is exemplified by the national courts of Germany, France, and the U.K. They follow precedents established by the ECJ, which has the effect of co-opting "the support of the domestic courts" (Garrett, Kelemen, and Schulz 1998, 150). As the highest forum for legal challenges, therefore, an extraterritorial court, functioning as the final appellate court, can play a crucial role in policy-making.

In the context of the British Empire, while colonies had no choice about the role of the JCPC, for a modern state to deliberately select an extraterritorial court as its nation's highest court of appeals is an extraordinary situation. If state sovereignty is linked to autonomy and can be defined as having specific capacities or powers that can be utilized without the consent or approval of another (Brown 2002), then relying on an extraterritorial court appears to be outside the very modern notion of state sovereignty. Since courts play an important role in governance and adjudicating disputes, the decision to retain an extraterritorial appellate institution such as the JCPC seems not only counter-intuitive but an affront sovereignty.

Elden (2006) asserts that modern states are anchored by three fundamental canons: "the notion of equal sovereignty of states, internal competence for domestic jurisdiction and territorial integrity" (11). These canons capture the tenets of sovereignty and the importance having the domestic institutions needed for supporting the state. The final appellate court is one such important institution. When decisions in the lower courts are appealed, the ultimate interpretation of constitutional elements and the adjudication of laws generally rest with a final appellate court (Aronson 2009). This renders the final appellate court a natural target of the other branches of government charged with making public policy. Capturing the role of the U.S. Supreme Court, Dahl (1957) stated,

> To consider the Supreme Court of the United States strictly as a legal institution is to underestimate its significance in the American political system. For it is a political institution . . . for arriving at decisions on controversial questions of national policy. (279)

For independent states, the JCPC's function is not [officially] imperial but national, with any limitations on its jurisdiction prescribed by each state's constitution (Beth 1977). While the JCPC can rely on cases from other jurisdictions as precedents, it is not part of a broader system or process of integrating the states. States have no control over any aspect of the JCPC other than the constitutional power to limit or abolish the jurisdiction of the court. Creating a domestic final appellate court, however, gives the state control over important aspects of the court including the selection of judges, terms of service, jurisdiction, and budget. This brings the adjudication of national policy within the state with the goal of making the court a more reliable partner in the national governing coalition. It is important, therefore, to understand more clearly why a state would accede to an extraterritorial court. The aim is to better understand these phenomena by examining why a newly sovereign state shedding British colonial rule and emerging onto the international stage would choose to retain the JCPC over which it has no leverage, rather than to create a domestic final appellate court.

The legitimizing process and the question of the compatibility of the JCPC with state sovereignty are exemplified in *M. B. Ibralebbe alias Rasa Wattan & Another v Queen* (1963).[5] The JCPC addressed these issues on the behest of the attorney general of Sri Lanka. The court is asked to address the issue as raised in a 1963 appeals case in Sri Lanka by Chief Justice Basnayake. Chief Justice Basnayake appears to challenge the existence of the JCPC's jurisdiction to hear appeals, asserting that the fact that Sri Lanka gained independence in 1947 automatically severed ties with the JCPC. The JCPC argues that the right of appeal was a prerogative offered by the British monarch to an independent state and that the parliament of Sri Lanka possessed the constitutional power as a sovereign state to modify or terminate appeals to the JCPC. Kelly (1994) notes that "there was nothing in the independence instruments to exclude the prerogative in relation to the Privy Council jurisdiction" (108). This point was not lost on the JCPC when it asserted that since its jurisdiction had not been specifically abolished by the parliament, the right of appeal persisted after independence. Cox (2002) conversely challenges the notion that New Zealand's sovereignty is compromised by having a court such as the JCPC as the final appellate court. In fact, he argues that it is a sign of political maturity. As these debates highlight, the decision of a state regarding the retention of the JCPC as the highest appellate court raises important questions about judicial power, state sovereignty, and the role of the judiciary in the national policy-making process.

Examining the case of the JCPC reveals important junctures in history when British Commonwealth states make decisions about the state's final appellate court. Further, the emergence and appeal outcomes of the CCJ as a part of deepening integration of the CARICOM further enriches this study. As the longest surviving regional integration undertaking in the developing world, the organization includes fifteen member states and five associate members bound by the Treaty of Chaguaramas (1973).[6] The integration movement is underpinned by four tenets: (1) economic integration, (2) foreign policy coordination, (3) human and social development, and (4) security (CARICOM n.d.).

The relationship between the JCPC, the British Commonwealth, and CARICOM, therefore, provides an appropriate case study. I build on Dahl's theory (1957) that the governing coalition wants the nation's highest court to serve as an ally and uphold its policies. He asserts that the U.S. Supreme Court is part of the national policy-making process and, for the most part, generally shares the policy views of the majority in the U.S. Congress. I argue that this is not coincidental; states not only choose the final court of appeal that they most expect to be an ally, but also extend this expectation to extraterritorial courts. While states may perceive some international recognition and prestige when acceding to an extraterritorial court, the governing coalition will abolish the jurisdiction of the extraterritorial court if it undermines or seems likely to undermine state policy. Examining this phenomenon across the British Commonwealth provides comparative insights into how states may view and interact with existing or proposed extraterritorial courts.

The JCPC is an example of an extraterritorial court with a broad appellate jurisdiction adjudicating for multiple states on appeals originating based on decisions of the domestic court of appeal. Though it serves as the final appellate court for many former colonies, these states have no role in the appointment, number, or terms of service of the judges, nor fund the court directly in any way (Howell 1979; Swinfen 1987). The JCPC hears appeals of decisions reached by a state's lower appellate court in cases based on domestic policies and statutes with the authority to affirm, vary, or overrule the domestic courts' decisions. Further, the JCPC's jurisdiction is not necessarily limited to any specific area of law nor constrained in its authority to adjudicate disputes between individuals or governments within the British Empire or those Commonwealth states that retain the right of appeal (Mohr 2011).

How the JCPC participates in and influences the domestic jurisprudence is evident in the decisions handed down by the court. In *Thakur Persad Jaroo v Attorney-General of Trinidad and Tobago* (2002) which deals with alleged infringement on constitutional rights,[7] Lord Hope of Craighead follows the precedent established in *Kemrajh Harrikissoon v Attorney-General of Trinidad and Tobago* (1979)[8] by Lord Diplock against abuse of the constitutional motion where there is a parallel remedy. This point is reinforced in *Hinds v Attorney-General of Barbados* (2001)[9] where Lord Bingham of Cornhill also adopts a position taken by Lord Diplock in *Kemrajh Harrikissoon* (1979) responding to a declaration for a breach of human rights. This is an example of the influence of precedents linking the interpretation of the constitutions of different jurisdictions over an extended period. It also demonstrates the JCPC's influence on the stability and continuity in these common-law jurisdictions.

Courts outside the United States have only been analyzed sporadically, and there is a need for macro or institutional analysis (Hönnige 2011). This research, based on the case of the British Commonwealth, provides a starting point for better understanding how states may respond to other existing and new extraterritorial courts. It is important to understand what states expect of an extraterritorial court, and how changes in the political environment of the state and decisions of the court influence the state's governing coalition, because of the increased attention to the role and importance of judicial institutions as a part of democratic institutionalization (Huntington 1991; O'Donnell 1973) and globalization (Slaughter 2000).

While this research examines a diverse set of factors that may influence the choice of final appellate court, some of the extant literature looks at the economic effects of the choice without analyzing the choice itself. They find that the type and duration of colonial rule significantly influence the subsequent economic development or prosperity of the state (Acemuglo, Johnson, and Robinson 2001, 2002; Crosby 1986; Gerring et al. 2011; Grier 1999; Lange 2004, 2009). This literature does not distinguish between the factors that influence the choice of the final court from other institutions after independence, however, and thus does not really provide insights into the governing coalition's expectations of the court as part of state governance. Voigt, Ebeling, and Blume (2007) focus on the courts and compare the resulting economic outcomes of states that retained the JCPC at independence with those that replaced that court. It demonstrates a potential causal link between retaining the JCPC and positive economic outcomes for those states. However, it does not help us understand states' choices to retain the JCPC at independence. The positive economic outcomes are identified after the fact with no evidence that the governing coalition made the decision with that expectation. The gap in our understanding of factors that influence the actual decision to retain the extraterritorial court in the first place remains unfilled.

To ascertain whether the governing coalition is likely to view the JCPC as a reliable partner or likely to undermine the state's goals, this research empirically examines the effect of several factors of colonial rule on the choice of final appellate court. This will better inform our understanding of what contributed to the perception of the court and the decision regarding its status. To best understand the JCPC, its link to the Anglophone states in the Caribbean and development of the CCJ, the book is important in its entirety. However, each chapter offers valuable details on different aspects of historical and jurisprudential development of the sample states.

PURPOSE OF THIS STUDY

At independence, Commonwealth states made dissimilar decisions regarding the right of appeal petitions to the JCPC that existed under British colonial rule. First, my examination of the history of these new states shows that not only did the decision at independence vary, what also varied was how long ties were retained by those states that did retain the JCPC. Examining the state's choice at independence to retain this extraterritorial judicial entity or to establish a national final appellate court will provide initial insight into why a state would choose the apparent compromise to sovereignty as defined by Brown (2002).

Using the case of the British Commonwealth, proxies for the influence of colonial rule on a state's decision about a continuing role of the JCPC at independence are operationalized. In other words, at this juncture, how constrained is the governing coalition by colonial influences of the U.K.? This addresses the path-dependent nature of institutional change and the factors that may influence any change. The persistence of the JCPC as the final appellate court for the new state is influenced by the strength of the colonial ties between the U.K. and the former colony. The strength of the influence frames the governing coalition's perceptions of the JCPC and these perceptions include whether the reliability of the JCPC brings prestige and legitimacy to the state.

Second, my research seeks to increase our understanding as to why some states decided to change the court while others continue to use the court, perpetuating the apparent affront to sovereignty. The findings show support for the assertion that the governing coalition is more likely to respond to unfavorable decisions of the extraterritorial court by abolishing its jurisdiction but that this response is most likely when there are changes in the domestic political environment that galvanizes the political will to act. This is more likely to occur when the state becomes less democratic or when the governing coalition embodies a new vision for the state which makes the extraterritorial court incompatible with the preferred policies. In these circumstances the governing coalition seeks to ensure that the final appellate court is a reliable partner in event their policies are challenged.

Third, this work contributes to our understanding of how governing coalitions view extraterritorial courts in the context of changing domestic political environments. Countries that have a domestic final appellate court have established a judicial institution over which they have control as part of the policy-making governing structure. How they view other existing and emerging extraterritorial courts will be influenced by their perception of the status of the court and the role it plays when the policies of the governing coalition are challenged. This book informs what contributes to their perception of extraterritorial courts in deciding to accede, how the state may respond to an extraterritorial court when it hands down unfavorable decisions, and how changes in the domestic political environment influence the relationship between the state and the court.

Finally, the case outcomes of those states that retain the JCPC and those that accede to the CCJ are compared. Specifically, it is asserted the state prefers a court that supports its policies specifically in cases where the state is party to the appeal.

SUMMARY OUTLINE

In the remainder of the book, I examine the choice of final appellate courts in former British colonies, with an eye toward understanding the expectations and responses of states to extraterritorial courts. Chapter 1 presents an abridged history and role of the JCPC in the British Empire and British Commonwealth. The goal is to demonstrate why this institution persists and the important role it plays in the jurisprudence of the states. It continues with an examination of the critical juncture at independence and a possible second critical juncture post-independence as the governing coalition responds to changes, if any, in the political environment.

Chapter 2 outlines the theory of high court choice and state building at the first critical juncture, independence. Dahl's theory (1957) is focused on the U.S. Supreme Court asserting that national governing coalitions desire a high court which will act as an ally to uphold its policies. This theory is extended in the research to argue that governing coalitions in all countries recognize the important role played by courts in national policy-making; therefore, decisions about court structure and design seek to reinforce this role in ways that benefit the governing coalition. It is further argued that states not only choose the final court of appeal that they most expect to be an ally, but the governing coalition may galvanize the political will to change a court that undermines or seems likely to undermine their policies. This theory is then tested in the case of former British colonies and the decisions whether to retain rights of appeal to the JCPC after independence is granted.

Historical path analysis contributes to identifying the first critical junctures at independence when colonies emerging from British colonial rule make important decisions about judicial structure and the goal to have an ally in the final appellate court. First, at independence, all newly independent states must design a new government, including the structure of the courts. Because former British colonies had to decide whether to retain the JCPC as the new nation-state's highest court, it is argued that colonial environmental factors significantly influence whether the newly established governing coalition viewed the JCPC as an ally or obstacle to policy implementation, thus influencing their choice of court at this first critical juncture.

Chapter 3 explores the relationship between the JCPC and the new governing coalition post-independence when a second critical juncture is possible. Changes in the political environment may lead to a disconnection with the JCPC after independence. If the governing coalition does not continue to perceive the JCPC as a reliable partner, a second critical juncture may surface. The JCPC will be replaced with a domestic final appellate court. Quantitative analyses using split population survival models, evaluate the factors which may influence the governing coalition to sever ties with the JCPC at some point after independence.

Chapter 4 examines the creation of the CCJ as part of expanding regional integration in sphere of the judiciary with the goal of providing an alternative for state to abandon the JCPC as a colonial relic and accede to the CCJ. States want a court that is independent of any single state but prefer a court that supports its policies. This is explored through a comparative analysis of appeals in which the states that currently retain the JCPC are a party with those that accede to the CCJ and compare the outcome with those of states that still retain appeals to the JCPC from 2005 to 2017. Results indicate that this simple measure reveals very little variation in outcomes.

Chapter 5 presents a summary of my findings and some projections on the future of the CCJ for the CARICOM and as a model for other regional courts. Outside of the context of the EU, CCJ is the only regional extraterritorial appellate court of its kind. The questions of whether its jurisdiction expands with accession of other CARICOM states, how the court adjusts to an expanded jurisdiction, and whether it remains an anomaly or template for other efforts at regional integration are yet to be answered.

In an increasingly globalized world, institutions that seek to meet the challenges of interconnectedness of states in the economic, cultural, and political spheres will continue to rely in extraterritorial institutions. This interconnectedness will also spawn the need for adjudication of issues between states, individuals, multinational corporations, and other nongovernmental organizations. Extraterritorial courts and other form of tribunals will necessarily play an increasing important role. This work, therefore, is a foray into a historical example of an extraterritorial court in the form of the JCPC and how states have managed the relationship. It also examines the emergence of a new extraterritorial court in the Caribbean Basin, the CCJ. While the chapters can be appreciated individually, the book provides a self-contained introduction to topic and sets the stage for further research into other extraterritorial institutions.

NOTES

1. The JCPC is an advisory body to the British monarch on appeals from the British Empire and former colonies that accept its jurisdiction.

2. CCJ, established by CARICOM, began accepting appeals in 2005 from acceding member states.

3. Caribbean Community is a regional organization of fifteen countries established in August 1, 1973, Chaguaramas, Trinidad and Tobago.

4. Lord Mackay of Clashfern (1927–) served as Dean of the Faculty of Advocates, Lord Advocate, and Lord Chancellor (1987–1997). He is a Conservative member of the House of Lords.

5. *M. B. Ibralebbe alias Rasa Wattan & Another v Queen*, 34 UKPC (1963).

6. The Treaty of Chaguaramas which established the Caribbean Community, including the Caribbean Common Market, was signed by Barbados, Guyana, Jamaica, and Trinidad and Tobago on July 4, 1973, at Chaguaramas, Trinidad and Tobago. It came into effect on August 1, 1973 (CARICOM n.d.).

7. *Thakur Persad Jaroo v Attorney-General of Trinidad and Tobago*, 5 UKPC (2002).

8. *Kemrajh Harrikissoon v Attorney-General of Trinidad and Tobago*, 3 UKPC (1979).

9. *Hinds v Attorney-General of Barbados*. 56 UKPC (2001).

Chapter 1

The Judicial Committee of the Privy Council

INTRODUCTION TO THE JCPC

From a few scattered outposts to encompassing large parts of North America, the Caribbean, Africa, and Asia, the growth and management of the British Empire is not just a military and cultural phenomenon. It is a bureaucratic leviathan that includes multiply judicial systems with the Judicial Committee of the Privy Council (JCPC) at the apex. This court adjudicates civil and criminal appeals from lower appeals court decisions originating in acceding states, colonies, and other overseas territories. This extraterritorial court is located outside the borders of the originating jurisdiction yet adjudicates appeals originating in that state. These states, colonies, and other overseas territories have no say in the appointment, number, and terms of service of the judges, nor fiscal responsibility for supporting the court (Howell 1979; Swinfen 1987). By this definition, the JCPC is truly an extraterritorial court.

The JCPC is a part of the Privy Council, which is a large advisory body that advises the British monarch in the performance of many ceremonial and substantive functions assigned by the parliament (Privy Council n.d.). Drawing its members from the Privy Council, the JCPC performs an important substantive function and derives its jurisdiction originally from a custom based on the medieval Curia Regis (the King's Court) or councilors to the king (*Merriam-Webster* 2015a). The JCPC's appellate jurisdiction is based on the theory that the monarch is the ultimate source and distributor of justice, but by 1660, this power only extended to all overseas territories under British rule (Burns 1984).

To understand the importance of the JCPC and the significance of the decision to retain this extraterritorial court by former colonies, it is important to delve into how it came to be such an important part of British colonial rule. Burns (1984) points out,

> The significance of the work of the Judicial Committee of the Privy Council in hearing appeals from Britain's overseas Empire and Commonwealth and from English ecclesiastical courts has long been recognized by historians and legal commentators. New Zealand's association with the Privy Council, which dates back to the first years of settlement, arose as a natural incident of the diaspora of the British people. For a new British community to which the colonists had brought their own legal system, there was no artificiality in a constitutional practice enabling an appeal at the ultimate level from the most distant part of the Empire, back to London as its centre and capital.

The modern roots of the JCPC are products of British legislative action and practice starting with the Judicial Committee Act 1833. On becoming Lord Chancellor, Lord Brougham introduced legislation that instituted several important features, thus creating the modern JCPC and replacing the standing committee referred to as the old Appeals Committee (Howell 1979). First, Law Lords had to be lawyers by profession unless otherwise specified by the monarch. Second, it established procedures and functions that were exercised independently of the monarch, giving this JCPC all the attributes of a court: power to call witnesses, deliver peremptory orders, mandate appearance, administer oaths and affirmations, punish perjurers, direct trials or retrials, subpoena documents, determine court costs, and punish contempt of court (Burns 1984).

Until 1844, the JCPC had no power to hear appeals without the granting of leave from a colony's court of appeal, usually comprised of the governor and the executive council. The Judicial Committee Act of 1844 (The National Archives n.d.) expanded access to the JCPC for the appeals of British subjects from all overseas territories. Under the Appellate Jurisdiction Act of 1876 (The National Archives n.d.), the Law Lords became the permanent judges of the court, and the JCPC evolved into the most important committee of the Privy Council. Today, anyone who holds or has held high judicial office in the U.K. or a Commonwealth country may be eligible for selection by the lord chancellor of the U.K. (Minister of Justice and member of the Prime Minister's cabinet) and the prime minister (Malleson 1999).

There are two categories of appeals to the JCPC: First, there is appeal by special leave from the JCPC itself as a right extended by royal prerogative. This may grant leave when the lower court does not have the right or has refused to grant leave. Second, appeal lies to the JCPC when granted by the lower court (Burns 1984; Robert-Wray 1966). Further, no monarch has ever ignored the advice of the JCPC in any case. Currently, the twelve Law Lords[1] of the court, sitting in panels of five or seven, preside over both criminal and civil appeals in London. The taxpayers of the U.K. pay the salaries and administrative costs of the court. Formally described as an advisory body to the monarch, it now possesses all the trappings of an appellate court of law. Modern legislative underpinnings leave little doubt of the judicial nature of the JCPC (Burns 1984).

The development of the JCPC was part of the growth and consolidation of British colonial rule around the world by serving as the final appellate court for the British Empire (Howell 1979; Swinfen 1987). Herbert Bentwich (1856–1932), a British barrister and law commentator put it this way: "[T]he King, the Navy and the Judicial Committee are three solid and apparent bonds of the Empire; for the rest, the union depends on sentiment" (Mohr 2011, 126). The exceptional reputation and lofty position of the court in the British Empire is encapsulated in its regal motto "Honi Soit Mal Y Pense" or "shame on him who thinks ill of it."

The contribution of the JCPC to the jurisprudence of the colonies and the Empire cannot be understated. This includes the thirteen North American colonies[2] that became the United States of America in 1776 predates the more formal and modern JCPC established in 1833 with the Judicial Committee Act. Though scholars dispute the precise number, more than 200 appeals did reach the JCPC prior to independence. One count is 265 appeals between 1680 and 1780 (Schlesinger 1913) and Smith (1950) reports 231 between 1696 and 1776. Further, the JCPC was already hearing cases from the colonies in Canada, Australia, and New Zealand. As the British established colonies in Africa and Asia, the jurisdiction of the JCPC grew accordingly with the authority of the Privy Council. For example, in 1886 the Settlement of Lagos (later the capital of the colony of Nigeria) was separated from the Gold Coast colony (later the colony of Ghana) by the Order in Council (Privy Council provisions in the Letters Patent of January 13, 1886). The Order also provided for right of appeals from the new Supreme Court of Lagos to the JCPC (Mwalimu 2007; Stafford and Wheeler 1901). For example, starting in 1858 when India became an official colony until its independence in 1947, the JCPC handed down approximately 3,750 decisions. During eighty-six years of colonial rule (1826–1957), the JCPC decided 347 appeals originating from Malaysia. Records of all cases adjudicated by the JCPC from 1809 to 2015 are available in the database of the British and Irish Information Institute (2014).

With the start of decolonization in 1931, the JCPC continued to play a role in the British Commonwealth states that retained the JCPC as the final appellate court. The number of jurisdictions declined from fifty-three in 1931 to just twelve in 2018. Despite the decline, this caseload is not insignificant. With a peak of 119 cases in 1931, the JCPC adjudicated a median of 47 cases (average of 52 appeals per year) from 1932 to 2017 (1,082 total cases during the 85 year period). The branches of law on appeal are broad and important with fundamental principles being adjudicated (Robert-Wray 1966). Examples of this diversity include extradition requests, constitutional challenges to the death penalty, libel cases involving politicians, eminent domain, personal injury, and issues involving provincial versus federal power. Further, the cases originate from jurisdictions with diverse legal histories and systems.

> Over the years it has been asked for final rulings and interpretations of many different kinds of law, from Roman Dutch law in appeals from South Africa, to pre-revolutionary French law from Quebec, and Muslim, Buddhist and Hindu law from India. (Judicial Committee of the Privy Council 2015, para. 2)

This rich and diverse history contributes to the positive reputation and the continuing role and influence of the JCPC in the common-law legal system shared throughout the British Commonwealth. Furthermore, the decisions set the precedents for the lower courts and influence the development of domestic jurisprudence. In *Thakur Persad Jaroo v Attorney-General of Trinidad and Tobago* (2002), Lord Hope of Craighead followed precedent established by Lord Diplock in *Kemrajh Harrikissoon v Attorney-General of Trinidad and Tobago* (1979) against abuse of the constitutional motion in criminal cases where there was a parallel remedy. The same point was made again in *Hinds v Attorney-General of Barbados* (2001) where Lord Bingham of Cornhill also reiterated Lord Diplock's earlier position in *Kemrajh Harrikissoon v Attorney-General of Trinidad and Tobago* (1979). This is an example of the influence of precedents linking the interpretation of the constitutions of different jurisdictions over an extended period of time (thirty-three years). It also demonstrated the JCPC's influence in stability and continuity in these common-law jurisdictions. Stability and continuity are important to the governing coalition for a number of reasons. First, support from the final appellate court can confer credibility on the government's policies. Not directly subject to popular will, the court may be viewed as an unbiased arbiter of disputes and challenges to the validity of laws and actions of the governing coalition. While colonies had no choice in the role of the JCPC as their final appellate court, newly independent states and their governing coalitions did have this choice during the process of decolonization when the colony gained independence.

DECOLONIZATION AND THE PERSISTENCE OF THE JCPC

Decolonization launches the process of moving colonies to independent states. During this process, an emerging governing coalition in the colony can decide whether the JCPC continues as the final appellate court or to replace it with a domestic final appellate court at independence. In 1858, Oxford University professor Goldwin Smith called for colonial emancipation and a severing of all constitutional ties between the U.K. and her colonies (in Howell 1979). Smith's assertion was derided both in the U.K. and in the colonies. This call, however, foreshadowed the process of decolonization that unfolded gradually after 1900. Although five colonies were granted dominion status within the Empire soon after 1900, it was not until 1931 that these five dominions[3]—Australia, Canada, Ireland, New Zealand, and South Africa—established themselves as sovereign states in the international community. It is noteworthy that only Ireland, having fought for independence (Dorney 2012), exercised the option to immediately server ties with the JCPC in 1931.

The process of decolonization truly accelerated after World War II. Starting with India in 1947, the U.K. introduced onto the world stage a plethora of new countries in Africa, Asia, and the Caribbean. The process unfolded relatively quickly continuing after India with Pakistan, Burma, and Sri Lanka (Ceylon), and with the termination of the U.K.'s mandate in Palestine in 1948 (Golani 2009). This was followed by the end of British rule in the Gold Coast (Ghana), Nigeria, Sudan, and Malaysia. By 1963, Cyprus and nine other African states had gained independence (Watts 2010). The process started in the British Caribbean with Jamaica in 1962, followed by eleven other states. These states formed the regional organization known as the Caribbean Free Trade Association (CARIFTA) in 1973, which evolved into the Caribbean Community (CARICOM) (Caribbean Community Secretariat 2011).

While most constitutional and institutional ties were severed at independence, arguably, the most influential institutional bond between the U.K. and the former colonies is the common-law legal system. This bond is not jurisprudence, and legal process, but institutional in the form of the JCPC. Some states such as Tanzania, Pakistan, and Sierra Leone abolished appeals to the JCPC at independence. Yet, despite the gradual process of decolonization that unfolded after World War II and the states establishing new regional ties, the JCPC continued to play a role in policy-making as part of the governing coalition in many independent states. The JCPC continued not only to be part of the judiciary in many small states such as those in states in the Caribbean, but also in larger, more populous and disparate states such as South Africa until 1950, Sri Lanka until 1974, Malaysia until 1985, The Gambia until 1996, and some Pacific states. For example, Australia and New Zealand severed ties with the JCPC fifty and ninety-five years respectively after independence. Others, such as Jamaica and St. Lucia, still retain ties with the JCPC fifty-two years and twenty-two years after independence, respectively. Today, there are still fourteen British overseas territories around the world that comprise the remains of the British Empire.[4] The British Commonwealth has fifty-three member states from Africa, Asia, the Americas, Europe, and the Pacific regions (The Commonwealth 2015, para. 1).

A preliminary review provides more insight into the relationship between the sample of fifty states from the British Commonwealth and the JCPC. A comparative review reveals that based on this choice, states fall into the three distinct groups displayed in table 1.1. The absence or presence of change puts the states on varying trajectories of institutional choices suitable for analysis to better our understanding of what influences the governing coalition and the relationship with an extraterritorial court.

Fifty former colonies are represented in table 1.1. Group 1 is comprised of the twenty colonies (40%) that abolished all appeals to the JCPC at independence. This group does not include the thirteen North American colonies that became the United States because they did not emerge as separate independent countries. It is impossible, therefore, to assess any possible difference in judicial outcome before and after independence. Further, the independence of the thirteen colonies in 1776 predated the more formal and modern JCPC established later as part of the expansion of British colonial rule. In Group 2 are the eighteen states (36%) that retained the right of appeal for a period after independence before abolishing access to the JCPC. The new governing coalition is directly impacted by the decisions of the final court of appeal only after independence. The decisions of the court may influence the governing coalition's perception of the court as a reliable partner. In Group 3 are the twelve former colonies (24%) that as of January 1, 2018, still retain the JCPC as the final appellate court. These differences point to competing approaches in governance and policy-making by sovereign states and to how states may view this extraterritorial court as a partner in policy-making and the approach to state sovereignty.

Table 1.1 The Status of the JCPC in Each New State at Independence

Group	*Relationship with JCPC*	*States*
1	Abolished appeals to JCPC at Independence (twenty states)	Botswana, Cyprus, Ireland, Rep. of, Lesotho, Malawi, Maldives, Malta, Myanmar, Nauru, Papua New Guinea, Samoa, Seychelles, Sierra Leone, Solomon Islands, Swaziland, Tanzania, Tonga, Vanuatu, Zambia, Zimbabwe
2	Retained appeals to JCPC for a period before severing (eighteen states)	Australia, Barbados, Belize, Canada, Dominica, Guyana, Fiji, India, The Gambia, Ghana, Kenya, Malaysia, New Zealand, Nigeria, Singapore, South Africa, Sri Lanka, Uganda
3	Retain appeals to JCPC (twelve states)	Antigua and Barbuda, The Bahamas, Brunei, Grenada, Jamaica, Kiribati, Mauritius, St. Lucia, St. Kitts and Nevis, St. Vincent and the Grenadines, Trinidad and Tobago, Tuvalu

Second, twenty-six of the thirty states that retained appeals to the JCPC after independence are analyzed. Subsequently, fifteen of those states (58%) abolished appeals at different times with eleven states (42%) retaining the JCPC on January 1, 2015.

As states emerged from colonial rule, therefore, there was a decrease in the number of jurisdictions served by the JCPC and a decrease in the number of appeals adjudicated. Figure 1.1 displays the decline in the number of states over time starting in 1931 (Act of Westminster) and the corresponding change in the number of cases disposed of by the JCPC from 1931 to 2017. The number of cases includes the states, colonies, and territories that continue to retain the JCPC. The steep drop in the annual number of cases from 119 in 1931 to 34 in 1950 can be explained by the fact that Canada and India abolished appeals to the JCPC in 1948 and 1950, respectively. After that time, despite the gradual decline in the number of countries from forty-eight in 1955 to twelve in 2017, the number of cases per annum increased from thirty-nine in 1955 to forty-nine cases in 2017, illustrating a continued reliance on the JCPC. Based on my review of JCPC cases, an uptick in appeals in death penalty appeals from the Commonwealth Caribbean explains the high point in 1995 with sixty-one cases. Despite the gradual decline in the number of states, those that continue to use the JCPC do so more frequently. It also speaks to the reputation of the JCPC and the reliance the states have on this extraterritorial court, despite the apparent contradiction with the ideal of sovereignty. As discussed earlier, the understanding of state sovereignty and the linkage to political autonomy (Brown 2002) is contradicted by the reality that many new states emerging from colonial rule retained the right of appeal to JCPC.

Using the British Empire and the Commonwealth states as case studies, this research examines the decisions of the governing coalition as the states emerge through the process of decolonization and the status of the JCPC after independence. My research covers a period of approximately 360 years, beginning with the declaration of the earliest British settlements as colonies and culminating with colonies that attained independence and the right to determine the fate of the relationship with the JCPC. The fourteen territories that are currently British colonies and dependencies are not included. This is an important and appropriate case for both theoretical and methodological reasons. First, the size of British Empire provides many states to study, as well as important similarities and variations across states. The states in the sample share the British common-law system, use of English as a common language, and colonial history and socioeconomic ties with the U.K. However, they also vary in important ways: land area, population size and density, demographic location, and socioeconomic conditions.

Second, the British were the first to recognize and enforce differing styles of imperial rule (Fisher 1991). This work, therefore, examines the influence of differing political environments. The British's goal is to impose efficient and effective rule and avoid resistance where possible. While British colonial holdings can be described in five broad groups listed in the next sections, they tried to individualize each colony's institutional framework to best adapt to the specific circumstances. The first three groups represent states that gained independence after varying periods of colonial rule and experienced direct or indirect formal colonial rule: (a) settled colonies, (b) dependencies, and (c) the special case of India. The next two groups, where the U.K. exercise control over the territories without formal colonial rule, are as follows: (d) protectorates and (e) mandated territories. Though the period of colonial rule varied from state to state, these groupings provide a uniform framework to establish comparable periods of analyses from which to justify my sample of states.

(a) The first group, settled colonies includes Canada, New Zealand, Australia, and the thirteen American colonies that declared their independence from the U.K. as the United States in 1776. Crosby (1986; Veracini 2013) describes settled colonies as those where settlers tried to replicate European institutions, emphasizing private property and checks on government. In New Zealand, an early association of the British Diaspora led to the natural constitutional practice of enabling appeals to the JCPC with the transposition of the legal system by colonists in a most distant part of the Empire (Haslam 1972). For them, with large British settler and small marginalized indigenous populations, there was nothing artificial about placing the seat of ultimate appeal in London as the center and capital of the Empire. It is safe to also extend this view to both Canada and Australia. A subgroup of colonial holdings was the original Caribbean colonies including Barbados and Jamaica. These were primarily plantation colonies lacking indigenous populations, with small British settler populations and large African slave labor forces. British institutions permeated all these colonies, resulting in what was later characterized as carbon copies of British constitutional practice (Juegensmeyer 1964) or what is generally referred to as the Westminster model of government;
(b) Dependencies were colonies governed by British imperial policy, which included defense and foreign relations. This group includes colonies such as Malaysia, Kenya, and Nigeria, where the purpose of colonial administrations was to transfer as much of the resources of the colony to the colonizer as possible (Crosby 1986). In these colonies with large indigenous populations and small British settler populations, colonial officers supported miniscule administrative-legal institutions concentrated in the

capital with little interaction with the indigenous population, therefore permeating very little of the social and local infrastructural power (Porter 2012; Mann 1984);

(c) The special case of colonial India describes geographic areas that were drawn into the colony via various means. Areas that were under the administration of local kings were incorporated by agreement or force. Known as the native or the princely states, the defense and foreign policies of these areas were entirely controlled by the British during the colonial period, but they did enjoy a substantial degree of self-rule in internal administration. Unlike other colonies, Indian appeals went directly from the provinces to the JCPC. India did not have a single appeals court until 1938 when the Federal Court of India was created under the Government of India Act of 1935 (Gadbois 1963; De 2012). As a result, India was described as "mixed colonial state" (McCartney 2015, 187) with regional and nation structures acting independently on some spheres of governance. On gaining independence in 1948, all areas were integrated into an independent Indian state with a standardized administration and legal system (Iyer 2010). Although members of the British Commonwealth, Pakistan, which was originally part of the Indian colony, and Bangladesh, which was originally part of an independent Pakistan (Hauss 2015), are both excluded.

The last two groups are territories that experienced British rule without the formal colonial status but via the status of protectorate or mandate. No territories from these groups are included in the sample of states because they are not recognized as formal colonies by an act of the British parliament but are included here to provide a contrast with the first three categories.

(d) Protectorates such as Aden, Nyasaland, and Somaliland were territories with no properly organized internal government. The British, therefore, not only controlled external matters, such as defense and foreign relations, but also established internal legal and administrative institutions. Britain's involvement in their protectorates was roughly equivalent to its involvement in the colonies without the status of a formal colony (Lange 2004 2009);

(e) Mandated territories such as Palestine, Iraq, and Transjordan were administered by the British Empire via a mandate from the League of Nations and were never formal colonies. These territories only experienced administrative rule for a relatively short period (Lange 2004; 2009). Fieldhouse (2006) characterizes these as collaborations being between the imperial power, the existing local institutions, and the elite after the fragmentation of the Ottoman Empire. Thus, they are not included in this research.

The growth of the Empire reflected the replication of British institutions in territories where no significant traditional/customary institutions existed, the local institutions were erased, or British institutions were superimposed on traditional institutions in colonized territory. Their effectiveness in replicating or superimposing institutions not only contributed to the number of states available for analysis, but also increased suitability for comparative research. The existence and persistence of a signature colonial institution such as the JCPC was a phenomenon unobserved in other postcolonial states that emerged from other empires, such as the French or Spanish empires. The growth of the Empire reflects the effectiveness of the colonizing policies and processes. From a few islands in the Caribbean seized from Spain, settlements along the eastern seaboard of North America, around the rim of Hudson Bay and Nova Scotia, and a few trading posts on the west coasts of Africa and India in 1746 (Porter 1999), it encompassed 25 percent of the world by 1914. The only completely successful revolution against British colonial rule was that of the thirteen colonies that formed the United States in 1776. Bilder (2012) suggests that JCPC appeals are the forerunners to the appeals to the U.S. Supreme Court enumerated in Article 3 of the U.S. Constitution. The Empire eventually included large geographic areas of Africa, Asia, North America, the Caribbean and its global trade included close links with South America and other areas (Lawrence 1996). The extent and diversity of the Empire and the large number of independent states that emerged during decolonization makes it an appropriate case for analysis of this appellate court.

First, the JCPC is arguably the first and most important example of a single extraterritorial court that evolved specifically for colonies, as no other colonial power had such a court. Further, the JCPC is the best example of a modern extraterritorial court. The JCPC is not just of historical significance, but it also illustrates the expedience of such a court and the integral role and influence of JCPC in British Commonwealth (Roberts-Wray 1966). The number of years the state was under colonial rule (from Crown Colony) is used to determine the length of British colonial rule before independence. This section explores the distribution and central tendency of this factor and shows the correlation between length of colonial rule and the decision about the status of the JCPC as part of the colonial influence. British occupation of a specific territory may have started much earlier. For example, the East India Company (also known as the English East India Company) operated in parts of India starting as early as the 1620s (Encyclopædia Britannica 2015), but India only became a formal British colony in 1858 (Stein 2001). Another example is Belize where British settlers started commercial logging as early as the 1650s (Mwakikagile 2014), but the settlement did not become a colony until 1840 (Borland 1975; see also Mwakikagile 2014). Also, Jamaica was seized from Spain in 1655 and was formally ceded and joined the British Empire in 1670.

The establishment of an official colony, therefore, signals the inclusion of a specific territory as part of the British Empire. This provides a definitive starting point for calculating the number of years the state experienced British colonial rule. The total number of years for each colony represents the duration of colonial influence on the local institutional development and is a proxy for how deeply embedded the institution is in society (Grier 1999; Lange 2004). The institutions are intertwined more deeply in the fabric of the society. Periods of official British rule for each colony varied from as few as 16 years in Myanmar (previously governed as part of the Indian colony) to as many as 360 years in St. Kitts and Nevis. The year of independence and the period of colonial rule from colony to independence for each state (The Commonwealth 2015) in the sample are presented in table 1.2. British colonial rule ranges from 15 to 360 years with some small colonies still scattered across the globe. The average length of colonial rule is 120.9 years ($SD = 79.61$) and a median of 88 years.

INFLUENCE OF THE JCPC ON CARIBBEAN JURISPRUDENCE

In addressing the influence of the JCPC and the respect it engendered in Australia, the words of the Honorable Justice Michael Kirby (2008, 13) is easily ascribed to other British Commonwealth states:

> First, there was the realistic appreciation that the same personalities substantially constituted both their Lordships' House and the Privy Council, so that a very high coincidence of judicial approach and conclusion was to be expected from each tribunal. Secondly, the habits of Empire inculcated in Australian lawyers a high measure of respect for just about everything that came from the Imperial capital. Not least in the pronouncements of law which was the glue that helped to bind the Empire together. Thirdly, traditions long observed and utility derived from linkage to one of the great legal systems of the world as well as the high standards of reasoning typical of the House of Lords, helped maintain the impact of its influence long after the Imperial tide had receded.

In 1961, the year before Jamaica gained independence from the U.K., there were eighteen colonies in the British Caribbean. By 1983, twelve more states emerged leaving six colonies in the Caribbean: The independent states are Antigua and Barbuda, The Bahamas, Barbados, Belize, Dominica, Grenada, Guyana, Jamaica, St. Christopher and Nevis, St. Lucia, St. Vincent and the Grenadines, and Trinidad and Tobago. The remaining colonies are Anguilla,

Table 1.2 The Year of Independence, Number of Years as a Colony, and if State Retained JCPC at Independence

Country	*Year of Independence*	*Years as colony*	*JCPC Postindependence*
Botswana	1966	48	No
Cyprus	1960	82	No
Ireland, Rep of	1931	120	No
Lesotho	1966	80	No
Malawi	1964	73	No
Maldives	1965	78	No
Malta	1964	150	No
Myanmar	1948	16	No
Nauru	1968	49	No
Papua New Guinea	1975	87	No
Samoa	1962	43	No
Seychelles	1976	161	No
Solomon Islands	1978	81	No
Swaziland	1968	66	No
Tanzania and Zanzibar	1964	45	No
Tonga	1970	70	No
Vanuatu	1980	74	No
Zambia	1964	40	No
Zimbabwe	1980	90	No
Antigua and Barbuda	1981	314	Yes
Australia	1931	141	Yes
Bahamas	1973	256	Yes
Barbados	1966	339	Yes
Belize	1981	119	Yes
Brunei	1984	78	Yes
Canada	1931	168	Yes
Dominica	1978	214	Yes
Fiji	1970	96	Yes
Gambia	1965	77	Yes
Ghana	1957	55	Yes
Grenada	1974	190	Yes
Guyana	1966	135	Yes
India	1947	89	Yes
Jamaica	1962	292	Yes
Kenya	1963	68	Yes
Kiribati	1979	87	Yes
Malaysia	1957	61	Yes
Mauritius	1968	158	Yes
New Zealand	1931	91	Yes
Nigeria	1960	60	Yes
Sierra Leone	1961	146	Yes
Singapore	1965	153	Yes
South Africa	1931	59	Yes
Sri Lanka	1948	135	Yes
St. Kitts and Nevis	1983	360	Yes
St. Lucia	1979	165	Yes

(Continued)

Table 1.2 The Year of Independence, Number of Years as a Colony, and If State Retained JCPC at Independence (*Continued*)

Country	*Year of Independence*	*Years as colony*	*JCPC Postindependence*
St. Vincent and Grenadines	1979	195	Yes
Tuvalu	1979	83	Yes
Trinidad and Tobago	1962	148	Yes
Uganda	1962	57	Yes

British Virgin Islands, Bermuda, Cayman Islands, Montserrat, and Turks and Caicos Islands.

The issue of the death penalty is exemplary of how the JCPC influences Caribbean jurisprudence. In looking at this issue, we are able to isolate pivotal cases which, on appeal to the JCPC, alters Caribbean jurisprudence. With all states retaining the death penalty as part of the law, the twelve former British colonies make up almost one quarter of the total number of states (fifty-seven) that have retained the death penalty (Death Penalty Information Center 2018). The Law Lords on the JCPC have significantly influenced this issue starting with the decision in *Abbott v. Attorney General of Trinidad and Tobago* (1979).

In *Abbott* (1979), the JCPC dismissed the appeal based on undue delay in disposing of the petitioner's appeal of the death sentence before Trinidad and Tobago's Mercy Committee. In writing for the JCPC, Lord Diplock declines to specify the measure to assess undue delay. Based on Lord Diplock's statements on the matter, it was clear that the court should adjudicate the matter later. The opportunity to do just that presented itself in 1982 with the Jamaican case of *Riley and Other v. Attorney General of Jamaica and Another* (1982). The majority found that they could not allow the appeal on the grounds of delay and set aside the death penalty in this case. They did point out, however, that their decision did not usurp the authority of the governor general[5] of Jamaica to exercise the prerogative of mercy and vary the death sentence on those grounds. The minority opinion reflects an alternative interpretation of Jamaican statute. The dissenting decision refers to the statement of the majority in the *Abbot* case leaving little doubt that undue delay would render the death penalty illegal (Ghany 2000). Ghany (2000, 42) asserts that this minority opinion is the turning point in the debate about the death penalty:

> *Abbott's* case, therefore, confirms us in the view not only that the period and circumstances of delay may be such as to put the taking of a the man's like outside the due process of law in other words, it is no longer justified by law) but also that the acknowledged proper practice of the state, so as to ensure due process of the law, is not to allow execution after prolonged delay.

Between 1982 and 1993, the JCPC allowed eight appeals against the death penalty on various other points of law. In 1993, with Lord Diplock no longer on the bench, the door he left ajar in *Abbot* opened in the Jamaican case of *Pratt and Morgan v. Attorney General and Another* (1993).

On January 15, 1979, the Supreme Court of Jamaica convicted Earl Pratt and Ivan Morgan of murder and sentenced them to death. They remained in prison for fourteen years during the appeal process. On three occasions, the authorities read their death warrants and transferred them to the condemned cells immediately adjacent to the gallows. In 1993, Jamaica's final appellate court, the JCPC, heard their appeal. The court concluded that this delay constituted cruel and unusual punishment and commuted the death sentence to life imprisonment. This case is significant in Caribbean jurisprudence as it is the first time the court has explicitly adopted a standard for cruel and unusual punishment based on delays in carrying out the death penalty. The court goes further by setting a threshold of five years on death row after which execution could be cruel and unusual punishment.

The majority overruled the decision in *Abbot* and accepted the minority opinion. They also incorporated Lord Diplock's dictum in the *Riley* case as part of their ruling which found a way to get circumvent the powers of the governor general to effectively prevent the execution on the grounds of unduly delay measured in years (Ghany 2000). The JCPC's preferences are made abundantly clear in the Belizean case in *Reyes V The Queen* (2002). Lord Bingham of Cornwall in delivering the decision states, "A generous and purposive interpretation is to be given to constitutional provisions protecting human rights. The court has no license to read its own predilections and moral values into the Constitution, but it is required to consider the substance of the fundamental right at issue and ensure contemporary protection of that right in the light of evolving standards of decency that mark the progress of a maturing society" (26). This implies that while the justices must follow the Constitution of the country, they are "required" to interpret it in the context of the times. Yet the court has not been consistent. Ghany (2000) points out that in three subsequent cases (*Guerra v Baptiste and Others*, 1996; *Henfield v Attorney General of the Commonwealth of the Bahamas*, 1997; and *Farrington v Minister of Public Safety and Immigration and Others*, 1997) the court has been inconsistent in applying the advised time limits. This inconsistency resulted in the commutation of the death sentence in each case but for reasons other than inordinate periods of delay set in *Pratt and Morgan* (1993).

The number of appeals originating in the states can also gauge the influence of the JCPC. The year before Jamaica gained independence in 1962 there were eighteen colonies in the Caribbean. By 1983, there were twelve independent states that all retained the JCPC as the final court of appeal at independence. From 1962 to January 1, 2018, the number of states still

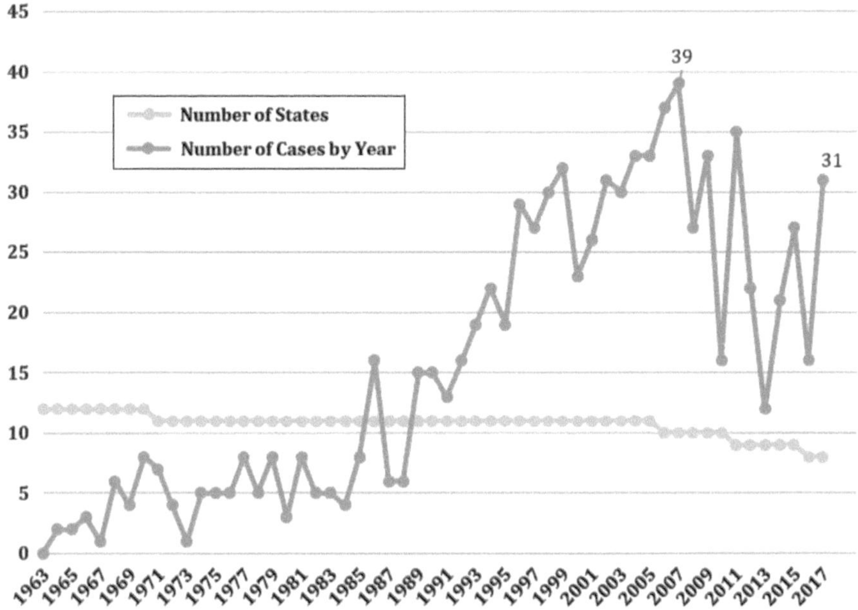

Figure 1.1 Number of Caribbean States Contrasted with the Number of Cases Decided by the JCPC.

allowing appeal to the JCPC had decreased to eight while the number of appeal increased from zero in 1963 to thirty-one appeals in 2017. The median number of appeals during that forty-two-year period is fifteen. Figure 1.1 presents the number of Caribbean states contrasted with the number of cases decided by the JCPC by year.

The distribution of cases varies widely by state over time. The tendency is for the more populous state that also has the larger economies to originate more appeals. The largest portion of the appeals, therefore come from Trinidad and Tobago and Jamaica who together account for 65 percent of the appeals or 31 percent and 64 percent respectively during the period examined. This must be qualified by the length of time the state retained the JCPC after independence. Trinidad and Tobago and Jamaica have both retained the JCPC since independence or forty-five years for each state to date. On the other hand, Guyana only retained the JCPC for four years after independence (1966–1970) with fourteen appeals during that period. Guyana went without a second level appellate court until it acceded to the Caribbean Court of Justice (CCJ) in 2005. The other countries to sever ties with the JCPC in favor of the CCJ are Barbados (2005), Belize (2010), and Dominica (2016). Figure 1.2 presents each state comparing the number of years with the JCPC postindependence with the number of cases per state from 1963 to 2017.

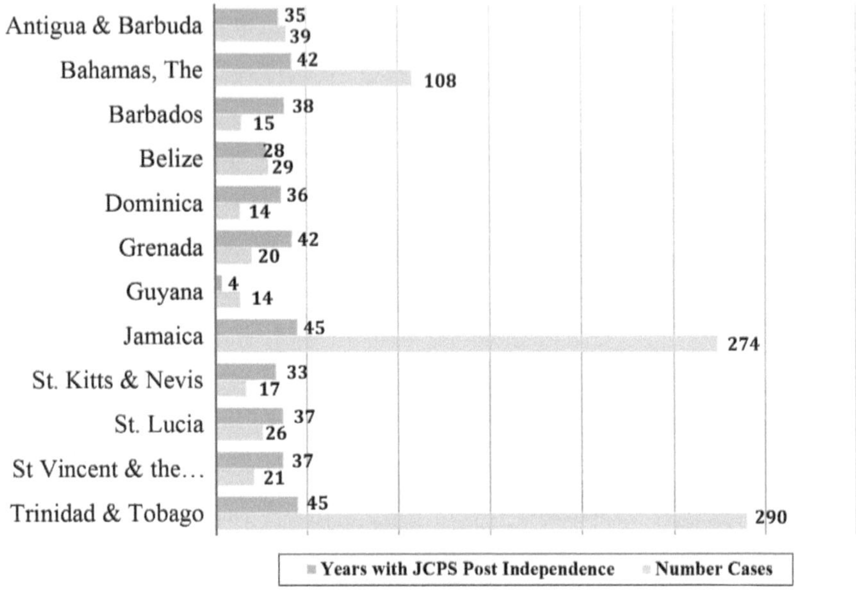

Figure 1.2 The Number of Years with the JCPC Postindependence with the Number of Cases Per State.

CONCLUSION

The JCPC was an important part of the expansion, consolidation, and governance of the British Empire. What makes the phenomenon of the persistence of the JCPC unique is that the U.K. made the court available to former colonies and that some new states did accede to the JCPC at independence. As observed by Lord Spens,[6] it continued to serve as the "great unifying legal influence" of the British Commonwealth (Hansard May 30, 1960, Column 95).

In the British Empire, the law Lords (judges) appointed to the JCPC view themselves as "umpires" (Ibhawoh 2013, 6). The role of the court as an umpire continues when the state retains the right to appeal to the JCPC. This effectively outsources the final appellate court to the former colonial power in an apparent affront the traditional understanding of state sovereignty (Brown 2002). There is no denying the judicial experience, quality, the prestige attributed to the JCPC, and that for some of the new states continued affiliation with the JCPC conferred some degree of legitimacy to their judicial system. The quality of the JCPC decisions are an important part of its credibility and the high quality of the Law Lords and their decisions are not seriously questioned in the literature. New states having not established an independent reputation for impartial adjudication would benefit from the right to appeal to the JCPC as it increases the credibility of their policy preferences (Voigt, Ebeling, and Blume 2007). This is exemplified by statements by the then prime minister Lee Kuan Yew of Singapore that the retention of the JCPC is a sign to the world of a commitment to judicial independence (Seow 1997; Tan 2015). The JCPC allows me to examine the influences of perceptions of the court, reputation, impact of decision-making, and the domestic political environment. The JCPC, therefore, illustrate how a single extraterritorial court can effectively adjudicate appeals from diverse independent jurisdictions.

As the data analysis show, most states of the Commonwealth Caribbean continue to rely on the JCPC as the final appellate court. The key elements challenging any change are the domestic political environments and questions about the independence of the CCJ. How this will unfold is yet to be determined, but Saunders (2010) points out that Lord Phillips, the first president of the British Supreme Court of Judicature, states that the JCPC spends a disproportionate amount of time on Caribbean cases and these states should consider having their own court. As of January 2018, the CCJ created as part of the process of regional integration and the alternative to the JCPC has only attracted four of the twelve states that retained the JCPC at independence. Ultimately, therefore, the influence of the JCPC in the jurisprudence of the Commonwealth Caribbean remains strong.

NOTES

1. President of the Supreme Court, the Right Hon the Baroness Hale of Richmond DBE; Deputy President of the Supreme Court, the Right Hon Lord Reed; Justice of the Supreme Court, the Right Hon the Lord Kerr of Tonaghmore; Justice of the Supreme Court, the Right Hon Lord Wilson of Culworth; Justice of the Supreme Court, the Right Hon Lord Carnwath of Notting Hill, CVO; Justice of the Supreme Court, the Right Hon Lord Hodge; Justice of the Supreme Court, the Right Hon Lady Black of Derwent DBE; Justice of the Supreme Court, the Right Hon Lord Lloyd-Jones; Justice of the Justice of the Supreme Court, the Right Hon Lord Kitchin; Justice of the Supreme Court, the Right Hon Lord Sales; the Supreme Court, the Right Hon Lord Briggs of Westbourne; Justice of the Supreme Court, the Right Hon Lady Arden of Heswall DBE.

2. Connecticut Colony, Delaware Colony, Georgia Colony, Maryland Colony, Massachusetts (included Maine), New Jersey Colony, New York Colony, New Hampshire Colony, North Carolina Colony, Pennsylvania Colony, Rhode Island Colony, South Carolina Colony, and Virginia Colony.

3. ". . . autonomous communities within the British Empire, equal in status, in no way subordinate one to another in any aspect of their domestic or external affairs, though united by a common allegiance to the Crown and freely associated as members of the British Commonwealth of Nations." Encyclopædia Britannica. "Dominion

British Commonwealth," accessed May 31, 2019. https://www.britannica.com/topic/dominion-British-Commonwealth.

4. Anguilla, Bermuda, British Antarctic Territory, British Indian Ocean Territory, Cayman Islands, Falkland Islands, Gibraltar, Montserrat, Pitcairn Islands, St Helena, Ascension and Tristan da Cunha, South Georgia and South Sandwich Islands, Sovereign Base Areas of Akrotiri and Dhekelia in Cyprus, Turks and Caicos Islands, and Virgin Islands.

5. A governor general is the Queen's representative and the constitutional head of state in a Commonwealth country.

6. William Spens (1885–1973), Member of U.K. Parliament 1933–1995, Baron Spens 1959—November 15, 1973.

Chapter 2

The JCPC and the Governing Coalition

INTRODUCTION

This chapter focuses on the JCPC as the final appellate court.[1] It examines the JCPC's relationship with the governing coalition in fifty British Commonwealth states[2] that includes the twelve former colonies in the Commonwealth Caribbean.[3] This is a broad approach to a significant sample of countries ($n = 50$). It is necessary, therefore, to make some generalizations as part of the meta-analysis. While providing a window into the relationship of the JCPC and former British colonies, this also sets the base for confronting more specific questions in other research.

The role and influence of the final appellate court, and those courts with the power of judicial review, on the policies of the governing national coalition are still subjects of debate in the extant literature. As the highest court in the judicial system, the final appellate court is the last judicial forum to which one may appeal for review of legal challenges. The assertion is that the governing coalition will want a final appellate court that it expects to be a reliable partner when its policies are challenged in court. In the relationship with an extraterritorial court, the governing coalition may not be just satisfied with working within the existing administrative structures but may move to completely sever ties with the colonial court. Variation within the fifty former colonies reflects that the governing coalitions responded to their colonial history and political environment differently which in turn decides the judicial structure at independence.

Courts function as forums for "dispute resolution," "behavior modification," "allocation of gains and losses," and "policy-making" (Baum 2013, 7–8). In other words, they are central to civic engagement about the constitution, laws, and public policy. First exemplified in a modern state by the U.S.

Constitution, the establishment of governing institutions and codified rights and responsibilities are now a hallmark of most state constitutions. The extant literature discusses the role and administration of the domestic final appellate courts in the United States and other states. Reviewing this literature informs my theory of the governing coalition's expectations of extraterritorial courts. Although Hamilton describe the judiciary as the weakest branch of the government (*The Federalist Papers* #78 in Bickel 1962), history shows that the U.S. Supreme Court plays an important role in policy-making (Howard and Steigerwalt 2012). Likewise, the power of the JCPC to rule on the constitutionality of policies or to adjudicate disputes with the state is important to the credibility of the national governing coalition, the legitimacy of their policies, and, ultimately, the effectiveness of those policies (Voigt, Ebeling, and Blume 2007).

This shift toward constitutionalism may have encouraged growing involvement of the courts in a broad range of issues, which is animated by an apparent failure or reluctance on the part of legislatures to address important policy issues decisively (Saunders 2010). All legal systems have a court of last resort as the final judicial authority for public policies, effectively making them "devices of centralized policy-making" (Shapiro 1981, 20). In many instances, therefore, the decisions of the final court are the last word on a given matter. The outcome is that the courts become part of the policy-making and legitimizing process. Furthermore, the decisions set the precedents for lower courts and influence the development of domestic jurisprudence (Lupo and Voeten 2011).

Given the courts' role and function as the final appellate court, states care a great deal about courts and how they are structured. Stability and continuity are important to the governing coalition for several reasons. First, support from the final appellate court can confer credibility on the government's policies. Not directly subject to popular will, the court may be viewed as an unbiased arbiter of disputes and challenges to the validity of laws and actions of the governing coalition. The view of the court as an unbiased arbiter of conflicts is supported by public opinion surveys. For example, the Maxwell Poll (2005; see also Justice at Stake Campaign 2001) in the United States found strong support for the notion that independent judges are unbiased protectors of constitutional rights. On the other hand, though driven by legal principle, there is recognition that the courts are political institutions (Bailey and Maltzman 2008; Keck 2007). Nevertheless, it is recognized in the extant literature that the U.S. Supreme Court does have the "power to confer constitutional legitimacy" (McKeever 1997, 161) on the policies of the governing coalition (Dahl 1957; Geyh 2006; McKeever 1997).

Second, when the court supports the state, it reduces uncertainty in the society about enforcement of laws (Voigt, Ebling, and Blume 2007). In a comparison of African and Commonwealth Caribbean states, Voigt, Ebeling, and Blume (2007) find that states that retained the JCPC experienced higher levels per capita growth indirectly attributable to enhanced state credibility in the realm of property rights enforcement. Third, the court's support can be particularly important for politically sensitive or controversial policies and can legitimize particularly salient cases (Dahl 1957). Dahl (1957) posits that the "Supreme Court is inevitably a part of the national alliance" that develops and enacts public policy (293). The final appellate court confers legitimacy on (a) the policies of the dominant majority and (b) the behavior required for the operation of a democracy (Dahl 1957). The court, therefore, is expected to work in consort with the national alliance. Lords Spens is more specific about the continuity and certainty the JCPS offers new states in terms of foreign investments and economic confidence.

The U.S. Supreme Court is the final appellate court that provides answers to important legal questions that underpin national public policy. The clash between President Roosevelt and the U.S. Supreme Court over key New Deal legislation in the 1930s exemplifies the role and influence of the final court of appeal in public policy. The Supreme Court declared several acts of Congress to be unconstitutional, which stalled the implementation of policies the executive and legislative branches deemed necessary to address the economic challenges facing the United States during the Great Depression. This exercise of judicial review, however, was a major concern for the Roosevelt administration. The power of the executive and legislative branches to replace retiring Supreme Court justices with justices who shared the policy preferences of the elected branches was crucial to resolving the impasse with the U.S. Supreme Court. A threat to enlarge the court and appoint additional justices had the desired effect. Justice Roberts changed his position on the legality of Washington's minimum wage statute challenged in *West Coast Company v. Parrish* (1937) and the Supreme Court subsequently reversed itself and affirmed many key New Deal policies (Carson and Kleinerman 2002; Currie 1987). Whittington (2007) reframes Dahl's position on the U.S. Supreme Court. He characterizes it as being friendly or sympathetic to the dominant majority.

In addition, Geyh (2006) points out that the court rarely used its power of judicial review in ways to precipitate direct conflicts with the legislative and executive branches of government. Between 1789 and 2005, only 165 Acts of the U.S. Congress were declared unconstitutional (in whole or in part) by the U.S. Supreme Court (Justia U.S. Law). In other words, over time the court took a very pragmatic approach in exercising its power of judicial review (Epstein and Walker 2014). Support by the judicial branch is characterized as increasing the "credibility of the government's promises" (Voigt, Ebeling, and Blume 2007, 88) and presenting a unified position on the policy.

Therefore, the governing coalition desires that the final appellate court be an ally against challenges to its policies. Thus, elected officials select judges whose interpretation of the law will not impede the policies of the dominant coalition (Tushnet 2006).

This raises the importance, therefore, of the relationship between the branches of government, including the issue of placing justices on the court, tenure, and jurisdiction. About court appointments, Dahl points out that "presidents are not famous for appointing justices hostile to their own views on public policy" (284). This highlights a key point of leverage the elected branches of government have over the U.S. Supreme Court. The procedure for placing justices on a court is widely discussed, and its importance cannot be overestimated (Baum 2013; Moralski and Shipan 1999; Steigerwalt 2010) but is only a part of the spectrum of administrative control that can be exerted by the governing coalition. The power to determine the structure and composition of the final appellate court is, therefore, important to the governing coalition, as it determines the relationship of the court to the other branches of government and defines how the court functions as part of the governing coalition. Dahl asserts that this relationship makes the court a "national policy maker" (565). This legitimizing role makes the judiciary an important participant in the national political and decision-making process (Dahl 1957) led and influenced by the governing coalition. The final court lends legitimacy to the policies of the dominant majority, which Dahl (1957) describes as the "lawmaking majority" in Congress (284). Further, Dahl asserts that "the courts are not long out of time with the policy views dominant among lawmaking majorities of the United States" (285). In other words, democracy requires that the branches of government are generally in step with each other and work to produce public policies, with the courts functioning as "political institutions working with legal tools" (Rosenberg 2008, 619; see also Dahl 1957).

While the important role the final appellate court plays in policy-making is recognized and demonstrated in the extant literature on the U.S. Supreme Court (Casper 1976; Feeley and Rubin 1999; Frymer 2003; Mather 1995; Melnick 1994; McCann 1986; Scheingold 1974), other works argue differently. The significance of this role is disputed by others, including Rosenberg (2008), Delgado (2008), and Klarman (2004). They, along with others, assert that the role is considerably constrained by and dependent upon the actions of the other branches of government.

This interaction of governing institutions is also witnessed in other jurisdictions besides the United States. The period of emergency in India from 1975 to 1977 during the rule of Prime Minister Indira Gandhi's ruling Congress Party illustrated this dynamic in another common-law jurisdiction. In one decision, the Indian Supreme Court rejected the objections made by the prime minister's legal counsel and found her guilty on charges of corruption, despite admonitions from counsel about the repercussions of not finding in favor of the prime minister. In another decision, however, the court sided with the government's disregard for the right of habeas corpus (Das 2007) to legitimize the actions of the government during the state of emergency. Hirschl (2000) finds that a comparison of specific cases in Israel, Canada, and New Zealand demonstrates that courts rule for the most part in accordance with the policy preferences of the governing coalition. It should be noted, however, that this research was not a comparative study of the actual decisions of the courts but a qualitative look at specific cases in the context of the political environment in each state. While the governing coalition may not feel significantly challenged by any single contrary decision, over time they may decide to change the court if it does not appear to support the governing alliance or if there is increasing sensitivity to the legal challenges adjudicated by the extraterritorial court. Maintaining this alliance may go beyond exercising control over the court through mechanisms such as the appointment of judges and delineating jurisdiction. In the case of British colonies attaining independence, the choice of final appellate court enshrined in the constitution is particularly significant. The role of the final appellate court was more than symbolic, as retaining the JCPC preserved a significant tie with the former colonial power.

Though the constraining influences are different, this position is echoed regarding extraterritorial courts. States have to deliberately accede to extraterritorial courts and can withdraw recognition at will. This might imply that the court may hesitate to thwart the policy preferences of the state. In the review of the role of the European Court of Justice (ECJ) in the European Union (EU), Garrett, Kelemen, and Schulz (1998) assert that the "specter of coordinated responses [by a governing coalition] will make the ECJ more reticent to make adverse decisions" (Garrett, Kelemen, and Schulz 1988, 151). Nevertheless, the growing partnership exemplified between the ECJ and EU member states and the role of the ICC when states fail to act (Chayes and Slaughter 2000) makes improving our understanding of the relationship between extraterritorial courts as final appellate courts and states even more important.

The abolition of the JCPC and the establishment of a domestic final appellate court to make a total institutional break with the U.K. are in keeping with the concept of the modern state. Each state, however, could maintain the status quo by retaining the JCPC. This choice by the governing coalition may have been an effort at securing their interests with a prestigious court they expected to be a reliable partner. Exemplifying this assertion, Dippel (2014) finds that the political leaders in British colonial settlements voluntarily abolished their locally selected assemblies after the abolition of slavery in the Empire in 1836. This effectively moved the settlements away from a democratic process, albeit with limited enfranchisement, to totally autocratic rule by the U.K. (Borland 1977; Dippel 2014).

In a study of former British colonies in the Commonwealth Caribbean, Dippel (2014) further demonstrates that governing coalitions chose this course of action to protect their interests and preferred policies from the influence of the wider population. As a colony moves toward independence, there is a gradual expansion of voting rights that brings more people into the governing process. The governing coalition, who were cultivated by and had benefited from colonial rule, may naturally feel that their interests are more likely to be protected by the JCPC that is a part of the colonial institutional structure. The role and administration of an extraterritorial court, therefore, are not any less important to the states that accede to the court than if it was a domestic final appellate court. The predominant consideration for the governing coalition, therefore, is whether the extraterritorial court is likely to uphold their policies when challenged in court. When states use an extraterritorial court as the final appellate court, they effectively relinquish control over this important institution in the state's policy-making and governance structure. The governing coalition risks having a court over which it has no direct control making the final judicial decision on challenges to its policies.

The final appellate courts in British Commonwealth countries can function as a check on the executive and legislature by delivering decisions that run contrary to the policies of the governing coalition. Extending Dahl (1957) beyond the U.S. Supreme Court, the court's decisions and the political environment are important when legal challenges are made to the state's policies, as the members of the governing coalition want the final court that is most likely to uphold and legitimize its policies. This is held because of the similarities in the historical background reflected in the political and legal institutions. The political environment influences whether states will change that court if it perceives a disconnection with the court. The governing coalition must perceive a disconnection with the court that is enough to galvanize its political will to change the status quo about the final court of appeal. This theory is applied at two critical junctures faced by governing coalitions regarding the JCPC in states that emerge from the British Empire. If at independence it is expected that JCPC will fulfill the role of legitimizing their policies, the governing coalition will maintain the status quo. If, however, at some later point there are changes in the political environment and the governing coalition determines that the decisions of the final appellate court reflect a disconnection with their policies, the final appellate court will be replaced.

Independence, therefore, is the first time the new governing coalition has input on the final appellate court for the new state. It is here that the colonial influence frames the governing coalition's perceptions of the JCPC as it moves the colony to independence or the first critical juncture. For those states that choose to retain the JCPC at independence, the governing coalition is then influenced by the decisions of the court and the political environment which may lead to a second critical juncture. Ultimately, states will choose the final court of appeal that they most expect to be an ally and reliable partner. Ultimately, they may move to change a court that undermines or seems likely to undermine their policies. The decisions of the governing coalition can be observed at these two possible critical junctures.

CRITICAL JUNCTURES

Mahoney (2000) defines a critical juncture as a point when a specific choice is made among two or more options. The juncture may occur after a period of path-dependent stability or continuity and represents a period when a clear change is possible (Capoccia and Kelmen 2007). Here, critical junctures present possible turning points when the court may no longer be perceived as a reliable partner in the governing coalition. Existing institutions, however, favor the perpetuation of those institutions; once a state has embarked on a course, it can be difficult and costly to change directions. In other words, history does matter to institutional development and changes (Crouch and Farrell 2004; Pierson 2004). Historical institutionalism uses the concepts of path dependence, critical junctures, and the salience of ideas to frame this course change. More precisely, dependent actions and decisions in the past underpin path-dependent institutional patterns and outcomes (Djelic and Quack 2007; Page 2006). Vergne and Durand (2010) describe these historical underpinnings as what links the past and the future. In practical terms, the colonial experience may influence the new governing coalition of the emerging state to retain the right of appeal via the JCPC. The colonial history and effect may constrain the choices and perceptions of the governing coalition about the institutions that are included in the constitution at independence. Some state leaders may expect that favorable rulings from the JCPC, a court not controlled by them, will grant greater legitimacy than a domestic high court. In the case of the JCPC, understanding what factors perpetuate that colonial institution despite the change in the political environment marked by independence is the key at this critical juncture.

After this first critical juncture, the new state and the governing coalition find themselves in a "new stable institutional equilibrium" (Bernhard 2015, 976). Over time, however, changing conditions and new developments can alter the course of institutional development (Vergne and Durand 2010). Streeck and Thelen (2005) describe this as "incremental change with

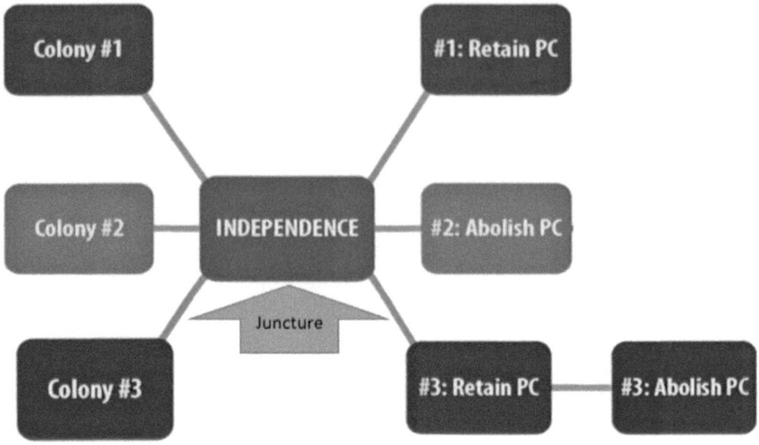

Figure 2.1 The Critical Junctures for Choosing a Final Appellate Court.

transformative results" (309). After independence, there may be changes in the political environment and the governing coalition's view of the JCPC's decisions enough to interrupt that status quo and possibly lead to a second critical juncture. The decisions made by the new states at independence, which is the first critical juncture, is examined and chapter 3 examines the circumstances that may lead to a second critical juncture for some states.

The first critical juncture for emerging states occurs at independence, while the second may arise later in the state's development. Figure 2.1 illustrates three paths colonies may follow in selecting a final appellate court, as well as where the two critical junctures may arise. At the time of independence, thirty of the fifty colonies in Group 1 in my sample perceive the JCPC as an ally and reliable partner and retain the court at independence. Group 2 with twenty states, therefore, do not view the court as an ally and reliable partner and abolish the JCPC at independence. The decisions of the new governing coalitions at independence are influenced by the realities of British colonial rule. The colonial experience underpins the path dependence influence on institutional development and changes. The colonial history makes a difference in making the ultimate break with the colonial power and the common-law legal institutions that existed during the colonial period. Of the former colonies in Group 3 that retain the JCPC at independence, some choose to form a new domestic final appellate court at another critical juncture some years later. This juncture is not inevitable, but seventeen states abolished the JCPC at various times after independence. This second juncture is a function of a changed political environment and a disconnection between the policy preferences of the state and the court after independence. In other words, political changes and uncertainty as to whether the JCPC will uphold their policies may lead the governing national coalition to view the JCPC as threat to the legitimacy of their decisions (Dahl 1957) or to the new vision for the state. At the point where the governing coalition perceives this discontinuity with the JCPC as an impediment, they may move to abolish the right of appeal. It is important to better understand the factors that influence the perceptions and opinions of the governing coalition about this final appellate court as an institutional partner.

This section discusses the first critical juncture in more detail. The closer look at the fifty states reveals a clearer picture of the realities of the colonial experience leading up to independence. Regarding the decision at independence. The states in the sample are placed into three categories—a states that abolished appeals to JCPC at independence, states that retained appeals to the JCPC for a period after independence before abolishing the appeals process, and states that retain appeals to the JCPC.

At the first critical juncture at independence, all states must design their new government structures, including the judiciary. Formal deliberations about the constitution for the new state lead to the first critical juncture at independence. Decisions about the judicial structure and the final court of appeal are part of the formal process of developing the constitution the colony will adopt at independence. This formalizes the framework for the executive, legislative, and judicial institutions to be transferred from the British authorities to the new governing coalition.

Reliance upon an extraterritorial court as the final appellate court for an independent state is fundamentally incompatible with the modern notion of sovereignty (Swinfen 1987). Retaining the JCPC postindependence, in effect, outsources the power of final judicial review to a court over which the state has no control. In The Gambia, this issue was part of the campaign to adopt the new constitution in 1996 that excluded appeals to the JCPC (Senghore 2010). Similarly, New Zealand's 2005 abolition of appeals to the JCPC was an election promise by the Labour Party. On winning the 1999 general elections, the governing coalition led by the Labour Party completed the process culminating in the abolition of the JCPC characterized as an important step in the national development of New Zealand (Wilson 2000). In supporting the establishment of the CCJ for the Commonwealth Caribbean, the former prime minister of St. Lucia, the Honorable Kenny Anthony states, "No self-respecting nation should allow its sovereignty to be at large" (Anthony 2003). More than half of all British colonies, however, retained the JCPC at independence. As of January 2015, St. Lucia still relies on the JCPC decades after gaining independence, while states such as Malawi and Zambia abolished appeals to the JCPC at independence. Other states such as Sri Lanka, Malaysia, and Guyana retained the JCPC at independence only to abolish appeals to that extraterritorial court some years later. There are two underlying questions.

First, why then did some states emerging from British colonial rule retain the JCPC? The effects and influence of British colonial rule is much debated in the literature (Porter 2012). On one hand, some argue the British rule was a net positive to the territories (Ferguson 2003; Porter 2012). On the other, some scholars maintain that while British colonial rule conferred important institutions and elements of modern statehood on the former colonies, it was brutal and repressive (Gott 2011; Porter 2012). As with all empires of the past, however, the influence lingers regardless of our normative interpretation. The British Empire is no different, and I assert that the influence is evidenced in the national governing coalition's decision about the final appellate court at independence.

Further, some states that retained the right of appeal at independence only later abolish the right, while others continued to allow appeals to this extraterritorial court. This mutability raises the second question. Why do some states ultimately decide to abolish appeals to the JCPC and establish a domestic final appeals court? It is posited that states that retain appeals to the JCPC at independence may later decide to abolish appeals if political changes increase uncertainty as to whether the JCPC will uphold and legitimize the state's policies. A disconnect may emerge over time that leads the governing national coalition to take steps to abolish that right of appeal.

The colonial period precedes the first critical juncture at independence.[4] The theory that the role of the final appellate court is the upholding and legitimizing of the policies of the governing coalition presents a better understanding of why some states choose the JCPC as their final appellate court at independence. This is tested using macro hypotheses dealing with structural factors (Rokkan 1966) of colonial rule that influence former British colonies as they emerge as independent states. The colonial experience encapsulates a variety of factors that affect each state differently in a complex and interactive manner. Length and type of colonial rule, period of independence, legal resources, and leadership each have an important role. The next section reviews the literature and explicates the influences that frame the perceptions of the governing coalition.

The establishment of a colony in territory effectively controlled by British settlers confirms total control by the Colonial Office in London over the political and administrative apparatus of that colony (Borland 1977). It marks the formal integration of the area into the British Empire and establishes the authority of the Crown (Dippel 2014). The legacy of colonial rule is complex (Porter 2012) and its influence multifaceted. The change in formal status embedded the colonial institutions in a colony to varying degrees and the effects of this undeniable legacy are still debated (Ferguson 2003; Gott 2011; Porter 2012). During the colonial period, a governing coalition was developed from the executive, legislative, and judicial branches of government and led by the governing elite. The governing elite or ruling class, which would make up the governing coalition, may include the senior political elite and bureaucrats, the leading members of the liberal professions, the growing bourgeoisie, and the leading members of the security institutions (Markovitz 1987).

Whether the governing coalition viewed the JCPC as a viable partner in the policy-making process of the sovereign state was influenced by the colonial experience that framed the composition and outlook of the governing coalition. For example, the cultural and ethnic makeup of the group varied on whether a colony was "settled" or "exploitative" as defined by Crosby (1986; see also Veracini 2013). Settled colonies were those in which British settlers tried to replicate British institutions with an emphasis on private property and checks on government power (Crosby 1986; McCartney 2015). The largest settled colonies were Canada, New Zealand, and Australia. With relatively small and dispersed indigenous populations, the culture and ethnicity of the local governing elite at independence were inextricably linked to their British heritage. This commonality may support the recognition of shared interests with the JCPC in maintaining the status quo after independence. As Diop (2012) points out, the institutions and infrastructure of the large settled colonies are steeped in the culture and tradition of the colonial power that are designed to maintain the status quo. This broad characterization of that group of former colonies contrasts with exploitative colonies. In colonies, such as Kenya, India, and Sierra Leone where the purpose was the movement of resources from the colony to the colonizer (Crosby 1986; Meredeth 2005), the characteristics of colonial rule and the effect on the emerging governing coalition varied. In African and Asian colonies, where the British settler population was generally very small, the local elite came from the indigenous populations and those of mixed heritage. The new local elite or "a new class of individuals exposed to aspects of European Culture that were super-imposed on the local ethnic cultures" (Diop 2012, 224) emerged as nationalist movements, usually culminating with independence. These colonies saw the rise of a "new bureaucratic class that was nurtured during colonialism" but which still had a history of tradition and customary courts functioning during colonial rule (Diop 2012, 224) making them less attached to an extraterritorial court, such as the JCPC, as the final appellate court at independence.

The Commonwealth Caribbean provides an interesting subset of settled colonies. With the decimation of indigenous populations (Caribs/Gariganu, Siboneys, Tainos, and Arawaks), the colonies were populated primarily by descendants of former slaves. Those of Afro-British ethnicity and later indentured Indian laborers resulted in "cultural heterogeneity" (Pramdas 1996, 9) producing "new native residents" (Pramdas 1996, 15) or in "creolization as a cultural mode of indigenization [that] is often rendered as essentially a single Afro- or Eurocentric standard" (Pramdas 1996, 17). Though exploitative in nature, Caribbean colonies were directly ruled with no indigenous institutions functioning in parallel to the colonial institutions as observed in the indirect-rule exploitative colonies. As with the other settled colonies, this subset of states retains the JCPC at independence.

The influence in the political environment of British colonial rule on the governing coalition's choice of final court of appeal is analyzed. Britain and its former colonies provide an important case study as it is the only colonial power to design a single court specifically for legal cases originating within her colonies, as authorized by the Judicial Committee Act of 1844 (Finlay and Walwyn 2008). As observed by Lord Spens, it continued to serve as the "great unifying legal influence" of the British Commonwealth (Hansard May 30, 1960, Column 95). The Law Lords on the JCPC viewed themselves as "umpires" of the Empire (Ibhawoh 2013, 6). The role of the court as an umpire continues when the state retains the right to appeal to the JCPC. Variations in structures and procedures notwithstanding fundamental aspects of the British legal system persist. Important features such as the adversarial and writ systems, along with principles such as stare decisis (let the case precedent stand), due process, equity, and an appellate hierarchy, are entrenched across common-law jurisdictions. The JCPC, however, also upholds differences between British laws and those of the colonies and states. The decisions based on the laws of the respective colony or state reinforces the idea of "otherness," which reinforces the distinction between colonizer and colonized (Ibhawoh 2013, 9). This is particularly evident in states with indigenous populations where customs and traditions are recognized, thereby supporting the tendency of these states to abolish the JCPC at independence. Still, decisions of the JCPC influence the development of common law in every corner of the British Empire (Ibhawoh 2013; Swinfen 1987), and this influence continues in states that retain the JCPC at independence. As heirs to the British common-law legal tradition, courts in other former colonies have a comparable role in national governance as described by Dahl (1957), and there is no reason to believe that the role of the JCPC varies from that of the U.S. Supreme Court. Specifically, therefore, I explore what contributes to the governing coalition that the extraterritorial court will be a reliable partner when its policies are challenged.

The next section discusses the perceptions of the JCPC developing over the colonial period generally and as a component of activities that are generally part of the decolonization process in which the governing elite participate. The length of official colonial rule was closely linked to the degree to which the colonial institutions became embedded and intertwined within society and the effect on the new governing coalition at independence. Lange (2004) finds that long periods of colonial rule lead to stronger state institutions that are connected to a broad swath of the society. This, he asserts, contributes to colonial and postcolonial development based on societal expectations that institutions contribute to the overall societal well-being.

The political environment the local governing coalition experiences influences their ability to identify with governing institutions. This includes their perspective on and degree of identification with the JCPC as a viable final appellate court for the new state. Iweriebor (2011) describes indirect rule having three main institutions:

> The native authority made up of the local ruler, the colonials official, and administrative staff; the native treasury, which collected revenues to pay for local administrative staff and services; and the native courts which purportedly administered native laws and custom, the supposedly traditional legal system of the colonized that was used to adjudicate cases. (para. 13)

Lange's (2004) assertion that the political environment can be represented by the type of colonial rule—direct or indirect—is arguably one influence on the type of final appellate court the state will choose postindependence, as the governing elite seek to establish the credibility of the new national governing coalition. Building upon Lange's (2009; see also Fisher 1991; Hirairi 2012) direct/indirect-rule theory, the works narrow the focus solely on the highest court. Direct rule permits local elites to run only the very lowest levels of the colonial administration, while colonial officials perform all other functions. Building on Doyle (1986), indirect rule entrusted extensive governance of the colony to the locals under supervision of imperial governors with both indigenous and colonial institutions functioning in parallel during the colonial period (Lange 2004, 2009). With the introduction of common-law traditions, the British still permitted considerable local exceptions in procedures and content in areas such as family, property, and criminal law (Hooker 1975; Mitchell, Ring, and Spellman 2013) in some colonies. Recognition of local traditional law placed legal power in the hands of local chiefs (Hooker 1975; Mamdani 1999), who exercised traditional authority over indigenous populations. The chiefs handled many disputes at that level concurrently with the established British common-law state level courts that typically supplanted the authority of traditional law. It should be noted, however, that the exercise of this authority was at the absolute discretion of the colonial officials and subordinate native leadership (Iweriebor 2011). At the time of Ghanaian independence in 1957, colonial laws provided for the operation of "Native Courts" in the territories of Togoland, Ashanti, and the Northern Territories that comprised the new state (Harvey 1962, 584). These courts were linked to the colonial legal institutions through three mechanisms:

(1) appeals to higher tribunals within the Native Courts system and in limited instances to an appeal tribunal outside the system,
(2) transfers of cases from one Native Court to another or to a Magistrate's Court, and
(3) review and revision of court action by District Commissioners or the Judicial Adviser (Hasnard 1960, 585).

In his examination of the Japanese colonial era in Korea (1905–1945), Kohli (1994) also acknowledged the distinction between direct and indirect colonial rule. He finds that the Japanese used both forms of rule by greatly concentrating power in Seoul complemented with a densely bureaucratic periphery and concludes that this provided the foundation for the development that occurred in South Korea after the Korean War. The type of colonial rule is closely linked to whether the colonial institutions became embedded and intertwined with the society. This contributes to the persistence of the institution after the end of the Japanese occupation. The governing coalition in colonies exposed to indirect rule experiences a duality of institutional structures, as customary and traditional legal institutions operates in parallel. This is in contradistinction to purely colonial institutions existing in direct-rule colonies. Kohli's (1994) findings in Korea underscore the significance of types of colonial rule on state outcomes. The type of colonial rule is likely to influence the choice of institutions postindependence. Indirect rule depends on collaboration with the traditional institutions supported by large indigenous populations that control regions with small colonial administrations isolated in the capital (Lange 2009). Alternatively, direct rule is characterized by dominant colonial institutions that are territory-wide and centralized, producing bureaucratic legal-administrative institutions controlled by colonial officials (Lange 2009). These institutions permeate where there are few or no indigenous peoples supporting traditional institutions. Direct rule is characterized by virtually complete domination of colonial institutions. The national leaders, therefore, view the JCPC as a natural extension of their embedded institutional hierarchy that brings credibility to the judiciary. These direct colonial rule colonies are more likely to retain the JCPC at independence. The type of colonial rule—indirect or direct—is important to the significant influence on the relationship between the governing coalition and the U.K. From the total sample of fifty states (former colonies), twenty-four are direct-rule colonies and twenty-six are indirect-rule colonies. Of the twenty-four colonies that experienced direct colonial rule, four (17%) abolished appeals to the JCPC at independence. Of the remaining twenty-six colonies that experienced indirect rule, sixteen states (81 percent) abolished appeals to the JCPC at independence.

The extension and imposition of British colonial rule, therefore, is inextricably intertwined with the institutional development of the colonies and with the perception reliability of the final appellate court as important to the governing coalition. Since colonial influences on this development culminated at independence, it is important to understand how the formal process evolved and how the colonies transitioned to independence. My examination of the fifty former British colonies extends this comparative approach with the focus on this specific institution.

It is asserted that the duration of colonial rule also influences the choice of the final court of appeal at independence. The average length of colony status for the states included in this research is 121 years. On one extreme there is St. Kitts and Nevis, which was a colony for 360 years before transitioning to independence in 1983 and still retains the right of appeal to the JCPC at the end of 2015. Zambia, at the other end of the spectrum, was a British colony for only forty years when it gained independence in 1964 and abolished the right of appeal to the JCPC. The difference may be explained by the lack of indigenous people and institutions on St. Kitts and Nevis which allows the colonial influence to be stronger over the longer period of colonial rule as opposed to the contrary situation in Zambia. The strength of the colonial influence contributed to the decision on the status of the JCPC. Only two of the twenty states (10%) that experience colonial rule longer than the average abolished the JCPC. Of the thirty states that retained the JCPC at independence, thirteen states (43%) experienced shorter than the average length of colonial rule.

The end of colonial rule marks the transfer of governing authority from the colonial power to the new national governing coalition who inherits the governing institutions with the constitutional authority to make public policy. The lengths of colonial rule contribute to the degree to which the institutions become embedded in the colonial society. This increases the familiarity of the new governing coalition with the role of the JCPC as more cases would be appealed during longer periods of colonial rule. This familiarity and longer periods of reliance on the JCPC increase the willingness to accept this colonial institution as part of the governing institutions of the sovereign state. The length of colonial rule contributes to the degree to which colonial institutions including the JCPC are embedded in the governing structures of the state (Lange 2009, 2004; Mamdani 1996). The colonial institutions have been in place longer and are more embedded in the societies (Lange 2009; Mamdani 1996).

The fifty colonies emerging from the British Empire are categorized by the type and average length of colonial rule experienced prior to independence and merely demonstrates the variation in the sample of states. At independence, sixteen of the twenty-seven (62%) colonies that experienced indirect rule, averaging seventy years of colonial rule, abolish appeals to the JCPC. Of the 23 colonies averaging 170 years of colonial rule, that experienced direct rule, only 3 (13%) abolish appeals to the JCPC at independence. This shows a greater tendency of indirectly ruled colonies to abolish the JCPC at independence.

I briefly discuss internal self-government and constitutional commissions that contribute to our understanding of the emerging local elite at this first critical juncture. During these processes, important national leaders emerged and led the colony to independence. My review shows that the first prime minister inevitably emerged from these groups of leaders (appendix B). This is important, as it may contribute to the strength of attachment the governing coalition feels to the JCPC.

During the first phase of the decolonization process, the U.K. grants colonies internal self-government. This process devolves the responsibility for domestic affairs to the locally elected officials, the emerging national elite, except for the responsibility for defense and foreign affairs, which remain the domain of the colonial power. The process of decolonization brings a shift in authority from the colonial power to the local governing elite and the opportunity to influence the judicial structure. For most colonies, the next step after being granted internal self-government is independence. The length of this pre-independence period varies with each colony but averages 14.25 years, ranging from less than one year for Zambia and Tanzania to as many as 75 years for New Zealand. Leading up to and during this period, the emerging national coalition is introduced to or becomes more highly integrated into the governing process and institutions. During this phase, therefore, with devolution of the responsibility for domestic affairs, the nationalist political parties emerge to contest elections. While these groups are neither monolithic nor homogeneous, national leaders do surface to take the reins of domestic governance. The background of these leaders may be significant, as they lead the local governing coalition's participation in the commissions and committees developed as a part of that transition period to work with the U.K. officials on the independence constitution.

The emerging governing coalition also participates in constitutional commissions as the second phase of the decolonization process. These commissions are instrumental in providing the framework for the local leadership to participate in creating the written constitution adopted at independence, including provisions for the final court. Constitutional commissions are comprised of colonial and local elite and serve principally in a supporting role to the legislative assembly. Their primary function is to provide expert advice on constitutional problems and issues in addition to proposing and drafting entire constitutions (Straum 1977). The goals are to develop constitutions that establish or strengthen the political community and to establish or amend the rules governing the state's power (Ghai and Galli 2007). Internal self-government is anchored in the Westminster model[5] of government and universal adult suffrage, with external and defense matters remaining the responsibility of the U.K. Considering the option of retaining the JCPC or establishing a new domestic final court of appeal is a part of this process. These commissions are significant in moving colonies to internal self-government to independence. This period of self-government culminates with the decision of the governing coalition about the independence constitution, including the status of the JCPC.

Lawyers are also considered to be a part of the local elite and influence attitudes toward the colonial institutions (Kelly 1994). Domestic law school as opposed to being trained in the U.K. plays an important role in the development of local jurisprudence and institutions. The absence of a law school would indicate closer ties with the U.K., making it more likely that the state would retain JCPC appeals. This has two aspects: First, if a law school exists in the state prior to independence it is likely to increase the number of local lawyers. This would support a larger pool from which judges could be selected for service on the bench. Second, locally trained lawyers may feel less affinity for British institutions than those trained in the U.K. Conversely, the absence of law schools makes the colony more reliant on the U.K. and contributes to the strength of the colonial influence.

As Acemuglo, Johnson, and Robinson (2001) state, therefore, the "colonial experience" is broad and far reaching influencing the development of the colonial settlements and the persistence of institutions (1370). While the colonizer and the colonized influence each other, the influence is asymmetrical with the colonial power exerting more influence as opposed to the colonized (Alemagung 2010). Further, "the political, cultural and general polity" left as part of the colonial legacy implanted "neo-colonial nationalist leadership" that led the colony to independence (Alemagung 2010, 64). These factors contribute to the additive effect of the colonial influence leading up to independence. This leads me to assert (H1) that the stronger the perceptions of reliability, the more likely the governing coalition is to retain appeals to the extraterritorial court.

COMPETING EXPLANATIONS

A review of the literature identifies three possible factors that help to explain why states might abolish or retain appeals to the JCPC: (a) sociocultural forces, (b) litigant access, and (c) geography. The research focuses on the states that retain the JCPC at independence then subsequently decide to abolish the right of appeal at different times. Further, the studies are uniformly qualitative and examine a very limited number of states without defining the causal mechanisms that influence the selection of the final appellate court.

Sociocultural Forces

Another explanation proposed by scholars is the incompatibility of an extraterritorial court with national ethnic customs and traditions (De 2012; Joseph 1985). Cultural and traditional differences are important in several jurisdictions where lower court cases follow customary law (Lange 2009) or native law and custom (Iweriebor 2011). These cases magnify the differences between the JCPC's administration of British common law and the administration of customary and traditional law (e.g., marriage and property rights) by the lower courts in the colonies that experienced indirect colonial rule.

Litigant Access

A primary constraint on litigants accessing the JCPC may be the cost of pursuing an appeal. Taylor (2005) points out that it is not difficult to start an action if one can afford an attorney. Accessing the JCPC, however, is not just a matter of being able to afford an attorney. It also usually burdens litigants with the costs of engaging attorneys in England to shepherd the process along. Litigants incur added travel costs and inconveniences just to appear before the JCPC (Swinfen 1987), considering the distance between London and many far-flung former colonies. Costs incurred are not only for local representation, travel, and accommodation in London but also for meeting U.K. visa requirements for entry into the country (O'Conner and Bilder 2012). Wilson (2000; see also Joseph 1985) concludes that some litigants' inability to afford the cost of appearing before the JCPC effectively denies the full right of appeal. Acknowledging this added financial burden on litigants, scholars have not established a link between costs of pursuing litigation before the JCPC in London and severing ties with that court. Former British colonies that retain the JCPC after independence are all far away from London and include some of the richest (e.g., Brunei, Canada, Australia, New Zealand) and poorest (e.g., Sri Lanka, Belize, The Gambia, Fiji, and India) countries in the world (International Monetary Fund 2013). It also should be noted that the cost of pursuing an appeal before the JCPC places a burden not only on private litigants, but also on governments with limited resources. A review of leading economic indicators (e.g., Heston, Summers, and Aten—Penn World Table) demonstrates that—apart from Australia, Canada, and

New Zealand—all former British colonies could be generally classified as developing countries, with many classified as least-developed countries (LDCs) in terms of gross national income, weak human assets, and economic vulnerability (Nations Online Project 2015). It also suggests that even if access was costly and only a few cases went to the JCPC, states expected to benefit from the good reputation of the court. In The Bahamas, which retains appeals, a former President of the Bar Association of The Bahamas argues in favor of the JCPC as providing assurance of a high quality and impartial legal forum for commercial disputes (cited by Rolle 2012). A similar argument was made by the chair of the accounting firm Deloitte Touché Tohmatsu on behalf of retaining the JCPC in New Zealand.

Geography

The large geographic distances between the colonies and the U.K. are connected to costs and credibility. Hogg (2006) concludes that the JCPC's shifting personnel and distance make it inappropriate as a court of final appeal. In 1943, the question arose as to whether the JCPC half a world away could adjudicate a situation in India better than a national judicial body based in India (De 2012). De concludes that the Indian Federal Court established itself partly by claiming a degree of authenticity based on location in India, in contrast to the placement of the JCPC in the U.K.

For the purposes of this research, the end of colonial rule for the dominions is marked by the U.K.'s Westminster Act[6] of 1931, which gave Australia, Canada, Ireland, New Zealand, and South Africa the option to abolish appeals to the JCPC (Swinfen 1987; see also Roberts-Wray 1962). The critical juncture for all other states is the year of independence, starting with India, in 1947, to the most recent Brunei, in 1984. In this chapter, I empirically test the colonial influences on the choice of final appellate court. The level of colonial influence exerted by the U.K. is operationalized by an additive index of specific features colonial rule discussed in the next section. My findings suggest that length colonial rule experienced by the state is a significant influence on the choice to retain the JCPC at independence. The higher index score points to a greater likelihood that the state will retain the JCPC at independence.

This analysis proceeds in the following manner. First, I explain the selection of former colonies for the sample. Second is the operationalization of the dependent, explanatory, and control variables. Third, the descriptive analyses with support of bivariate and multivariable probit regressions are used to test the theory on the sample of fifty states is explicated. Finally, the results of the tests, analyses, and summary conclusions are presented.

UNIT OF ANALYSIS AND SAMPLE OF STATES

The unit of analysis is the former colony or the state. Fifty former British colonies make up the "risk set," or sample, from the entire group of colonies and territories in the British Empire. Fifty former colonies are analyzed from the year of the official start of colonial rule to the year of independence. In effect, the analysis starts the beginning of British colonial administration with St. Kitts in 1623 and ends in 2014, which would be the last year in this analysis that a colony could gain independence. This spans a total of 391 years. For each, observations are made in the year the colony became an independent state. Importantly, there is the accessibility of high quality data from primary and secondary sources (Gerring et al. 2011).

The diversity of the British Empire poses a potential problem for unit homogeneity. This cross-regional comparison of analytically distinct units may cause inaccuracies in the results (Lange 2009). To increase unit homogeneity, I am partially guided by Lange (2009), who excludes the following categories of colonies: (a) hybrids that merged into other non-British territories, (b) internal colonies or those adjacent territories (e.g., Northern Ireland) conquered by the English, (c) British Mandates in the Middle East, and (d) other Middle East territories governed by the British for only a very short period. Lange in examining economic outcomes and considered the economic development, excludes Canada, Australia, Ireland, and New Zealand as distinct from other British colonies who each had the option to abolish the JCPC under the Westminster Act of 1931. These states are included in this sample. This is appropriate for this research because those states faced the same critical juncture in 1931 as other states in the sample faced at independence. Everyone had the option to abolish ties with the JCPC and establish a domestic final appellate court but only Ireland took the opportunity. The assumption is that for the purposes of this analysis the colonial influences and historical factors at work are similar enough to include them in the risk set. States included, therefore, are only those overseas colonies recognized as part of the British Empire by an act of the British parliament.

EXPLORING THE DECISION TO RETAIN THE JCPC AT INDEPENDENCE

As discussed, the predominant consideration for the governing coalition is whether the final appellate court is likely to uphold their policies when challenged in court. The loosening of colonial rule starting in the 1930s, results in a nationalism that results in self-rule during the period leading up independence (Furedi 1994). The governing coalitions emerge from elections contested by political parties that formed out of the nationalist movements during this period. This is observed in all states and clearly exemplified in Belize where The Peoples United Party (PUP) defeated the National Independence Party (NIP) in four elections leading up to independence in 1981. The leader of the PUP, Honorable George Cadle Price became the first prime minister. The theory is that the new governing coalition at independence desires a final appellate court that will support their policies and contribute legitimacy with the reputation and prestige of the court as they take responsibility for the peace, order and good government (POGG) of the new state. The perception of the JCPC as a reliable partner and legitimizing factor is influenced by the colonial rule experienced by the state. The decision at the critical juncture of independence is whether to retain appeals to the JCPC or establish a domestic final appellate court. This decision is influenced by the colonial experience of the state, which influences how strong the ties are to the U.K., which then influences the decision.

To test my central hypotheses, therefore, I estimate a multivariable probit model.[7] The model employs the additive variable (Influence of the Colonial Power) with four control variables. In the next sections I explicate the dependent variable and the independent variables.

The dependent binary variable for both models is whether the colony retains or abolishes appeals to the JCPC. The right of appeal to the JCPC is either explicitly provided for in the constitution of the state at independence or there is no such provision. In other words, does the "event" occur at independence? The binary variable is appropriate as there is no nuanced variation to be captured. If the JCPC is retained at independence the variable is coded "0" and if abolished it is coded "1." Of the fifty states in the sample risk set, thirty (60%) of the states retain the JCPC at independence while twenty (40%) of the states abolish appeals to the JCPC.

To examine the decision of the states about whether to retain or abolish the JCPC, an additive index variable is created to capture the effects of colonial rule. The stronger the colonial ties of the newly independent state to its colonial past and the influence of the U.K., the increased likelihood that the JCPC will be retained at independence. The goal is to capture more effectively the broad concept of colonial rule and its influence on the new governing coalition, which may not be captured by any one single proxy. An additive index is most appropriate when individual factors do not measure the effect of the entire concept (Ethridge 2002). Based on the additive model in Corley, Steigerwalt, and Ward (2013),[8] my additive index is scaled zero to four with states that experience the weakest colonial influence at zero and those with the highest scoring four (0-Low, 1-Med-low, 2-Medium, 3-Med-high, 4-High). A higher score reflects a great level of colonial influence on the governing coalitions' perception of the JCPC's reliability and advantages resulting in closer ties to the U.K. This may provide some insight into why the state may accede to an extraterritorial court. The additive indexed variable is comprised of the four discrete factors: (1) length of British colonial rule, (2) type of colonial rule, (3) tertiary education of leader at independence, and (4) whether the state had a law school. I discuss each in this order.

(1) The length of British colonial rule is determined by how long the state experienced formal British colonial rule before independence. This section explores the distribution and central tendency of this factor and shows the correlation between length of colonial rule and the decision about the status of the JCPC as part of the colonial influence. British occupation of a specific territory may have started much earlier. For example, the East India Company (also known as the English East India Company) operated in parts of India starting as early as the 1620s (Encyclopædia Britannica 2015), but India only became a formal British colony in 1858 (CiteHR, n.d.). Another example is Belize where British settlers started commercial logging as early as the 1650s (Belize.com 2015; Mwakikagile 2014), but the settlement did not become a colony until 1840 (Borland 1975; see also Mwakikagile 2014). The establishment of an official colony, therefore, signals the inclusion of a specific territory as part of the British Empire. This provides a definitive starting point for calculating the number of years the state experienced British colonial rule. The total number of years for each colony represents the duration of colonial influence on the local institutional development and is a proxy for how deeply embedded the institution is in society (Grier 1999; Lange 2004). The institutions are more intertwined in the fabric of the society. I expect, therefore, that the influence of colonial rule grows stronger over time making more likely that retaining the JCPC would not be viewed as a threat to the new governing coalition at independence who are more likely to view the link with the U.K. institution as adding credibility to the new state.

Periods of official British rule for each colony varied from as few as 16 years in Myanmar (previously governed as part of the Indian colony) to as many as 360 years in St. Kitts and Nevis. The length of British colonial rule ranges from 15 to 360 years, with an average length of 120.9 years (SD = 79.61). Based on the length of colonial rule for each state, the average length of colonial rule for the states in each group is calculated. The fifty states disaggregated into four categories with the designated average number of years of colonial rule. Twenty (38%) states with an average of seventy years of colonial rule abolished the JCPC at independence. Seventeen (34%) states averaging 106 years of colonial rule retained the JCPC at independence but abolished appeals at some time after. As of January 1, 2016, thirteen (26%) states retain appeals to the JCPC. Those states averaged 214 years of colonial rule.

The number of years the state experienced colonial rule is coded as "1" if the state was under colonial rule above and "0" if it was below the sample median of eighty-nine years. When the right of appeal to the JCPC is not abolished, average length of British colonial rule is 148.27 (*SD* = 88.34). When abolished, the average length of British colonial rule is 79.95 (*SD* = 38.55). These findings suggest that the less time a state spends under British colonial rule, the more likely it is to sever ties with the JCPC at independence. There is a central tendency of states below the sample median having experienced colonial ties for a shorter period would have weaker ties with the U.K. and are therefore less likely to retain JCPC appeals. I expect longer periods of colonial rule to have the opposite effect. Over time the governing elite will become more attached to the prestige and reputation of the JCPC increasing the likelihood that the state will retain the JCPC.

(2) This section explores the type of colonial rule—direct or indirect colonial rule—and the distribution and the central tendency of this factor. It shows the correlation between the type of colonial rule and the decision about the status of the JCPC as part of the colonial influence. Direct rule is defined as colonial institutions permeating the colony to the exclusion of customary and traditional institutions, with locals only participating at the lower levels of the colonial administration. Indirect rule is defined as having extensive governance of the colony entrusted to the locals under supervision of British governors, with both indigenous and colonial institutions functioning in parallel during the colonial period (Lange 2004 2009). Table 3.3 displays status of the JCPC with regard to each state—the number of states who abolished the JCPC at independence, retained ties for a period of time after independence or those that still retain the JCPC as of January 1, 2017

As Iweriebo (2011) points out, the system of courts using native and customary law were established as a pillar of indirect rule. Since the focus is on legal institutions, the indirect-direct-rule variable is operationalized using the percentage of total court cases following customary law (Lange 2009). Adopting Lange's definition, the indirect-direct rule is not dichotomous but on a spectrum. The percentage of total court cases adjudicated using customary or traditional law is a proxy for the extent to which the colony experienced the imposition of colonial judicial institutions concurrently with customary and tradition institutions. The percentage of cases adjudicated under traditional and customary law at the time of independence are as follows: Customary Law (Lange 2009) = 0 percent (23 states), Customary Law Cases[9] 1 percent > 50 percent (7 states), and Customary Law Cases[10] 51 percent > 100 percent (20 states).

This is operationalized by the percentage of total court cases in each colony following customary or traditional law (Lange 2009). There is a continuous variable starting at 0 for colonies where no cases were adjudicated using customary/traditional law to 100 percent if all cases were adjudicated using customary/traditional law of the colony. This variable ranges from 0 to 93 percent, with a median of 39 percent (*SD* = 30%). For example, in Canada,

The Bahamas, and New Zealand no cases were adjudicated using customary or traditional law, indicating that only colonial institutions made up the governing structures. In Nigeria colonial and indigenous institutions operated contemporaneously with 93 percent of the cases adjudicated using customary or traditional law. In other colonies, such as India and Botswana, the use of customary or traditional law is closer to 50 percent.

In twenty-five (50%) of the fifty states, the percentage of total court cases following customary or traditional law is above the average of 32 percent and thirteen (52%) retain appeals to the JCPC at independence. Of the twenty-five states below the average of 32 percent, eighteen states (88%) retain appeals to the JCPC at independence. The type of colonial rule operationalized by the percentage of cases adjudicated using customary/traditional law. There is a central tendency of states that experienced higher levels of indirect colonial rule above the median of 39 percent to replace the JCPC at independence. When the state decides to retain the JCPC, the average percentage of total court cases following customary law is 0.23 (*SD* = 0.30).

When the state decides to abolish appeals to the JCPC, the average percentage of total court cases following customary law is 0.46 (*SD* = 0.26). This shows that the average percentage of total court cases following customary law is significantly higher in the states that abolish appeals to the JCPC. These findings suggest that the higher the percentage of cases adjudicated under customary or traditional law, the more likely it is that the state will abolish appeals to the JCPC. States above the sample average indicate weaker ties with the U.K. as the presence of colonial institutions would be less pervasive in the population and, therefore, less likely to retain JCPC. The opposite effect is expected if the percentage is below the sample average.

(3) As the colony moves toward independence and as part of the decolonization process, the U.K. grants colonies internal self-government under the leadership of the new governing coalition. This section explores the distribution and central tendency of this factor and shows the correlation between where the leader received tertiary education and the decision about the status of the JCPC as part of the colonial influence. The leader who eventually becomes prime minister at independence is used as a proxy for an affinity of the governing coalition for British institutions by those leaders educated in the U.K. This variable, therefore, represents whether the prime minister of each former colony at independence was educated in the U.K. This control variable is dichotomous for whether the leaders received tertiary or professional education in the U.K. (1) or not (0). Nineteen states had initial prime ministers who were educated in the U.K. (38%). Of those nineteen states, fifteen (79%) retain appeals to the JCPC at independence. Of the remaining thirty-one states with prime ministers who were not educated in the U.K., 55 percent (*N* = 17) retain appeals to the JCPC. The difference (24% points)

indicates the propensity for those leaders educated in the U.K. to be more inclined to champion the retention of appeals to the JCPC. Further, there is a central tendency of states where the leader was educated in the U.K. to retain the JCPC at independence. A U.K. education may increase the willingness of a new governing coalition to accept an extraterritorial court as a final court of appeal. Returning to lead the colony to independence, these leaders appear more likely to influence the governing coalition to retain appeals to the JCPC.

Domestic law schools play an important role in the development and practice of law, resulting in the local jurisprudence. Lawyers are also considered to be a part of the local elite and influence attitudes toward the colonial institutions (Kelly 1994). In discussing the British colonial attitudes toward training lawyers, Kelly states of those with lawyers who "qualified in English law, that usually sealed the fate of the Privy Council jurisdiction" (107). The absence of a law school would indicate closer ties with the U.K., making it more likely that the state would retain JCPC appeals. This has two aspects: First, if a law school exists in the state prior to independence it is likely to increase the number of local lawyers. This would support a larger pool from which judges could be selected for service on the bench. Second, locally trained lawyers may feel less affinity for British institutions than those trained in the U.K. Conversely, the absence of law schools makes the colony more reliant on the U.K. and contributes to the strength of the colonial influence. While Kelly is only referring to lawyers educated in the U.K., it may provide some broader support for the result that leaders educated in the U.K. are more likely to want to move away from colonial institutions at independence.

If the state had at least one law school at independence, it was coded for the presence or lack of a law school. Of the fifty states in the sample, twenty had at least one law school at independence. Law schools contribute to the pool of qualified people for appointment to the bench. Due to distance and costs, relying of law school outside the colony restricts access and limits the number of local people able to attend law school. The presence of a law school, therefore, contributes to the local judiciary and may decrease a perceived need to rely on the JCPC as adding to the credibility of the judiciary. Of the twenty states with law schools at independence, fifteen (75%) retain appeals to the JCPC. Of the thirty states with no law school at independence, sixteen (53%) retain appeals to the JCPC. There is, however, no central tendency of states with law schools to abolish ties with the JCPC.

The indexing of these proxies for colonial rule provides me with a single score for each state in the sample. Of those states that experience medium-high (eight states) or high levels (seven states) of colonial influence, 88 percent and 86 percent, respectively, retain the JCPC. Of those states that experience medium (eleven states), medium-low (nineteen states), and low (five states), 64 percent, 58 percent, and 40 percent retain appeals to the JCPC at independence. This indicates the stronger tendency of states at and above the medium level of colonial influence to retain the JCPC. The results show the percentage of states that retain the JCPC in their constitutions at independence at each level of the scale of the additive index.

A bivariate probit model uses the additive indexed variable—*Colonial Influence*. The dependent variable is whether the state abolished the JCPC at independence, and the independent variable is the level of colonial influence at independence. The results of a bivariate probit regression displayed in table 2.1 show that the strength of the colonial influence is significantly (*p-value* = 0.009) associated with the choice to retain appeals to the JCPC. In other words, this provides further support for my theory that the stronger the colonial influence, the more likely the governing coalition will view the JCPC as a reliable partner in policy-making. Further, the governing coalition view of the prestige and reputation of the JCPC may be enhanced by the stronger colonial influence and increase the likelihood of retaining right of appeal to the JCPC at independence.

The first control variable is access to the JCPC. The litigants from disparate regions of the world bear the cost of appearing in a court located in the U.K. These costs may impede both private litigants and the state from accessing the JCPC. The costs may also influence the decision to establish a national final appellate court to reduce costs and increase access. Access is operationalized using the Gross Domestic Product (GDP[11]) per capita of each colony in the year of independence. The estimate of the GDP per capita for each colony is in U.S. dollars and is calculated in the year of independence (The Maddison-Project 2013). The distribution of GDP per capita of the colonies at independence varies widely, from as low as U.S. $625.00 in Myanmar to U.S. $37,806.00 in Brunei at the upper limit. The approach provides a basis to compare the advantage the more prosperous states may have over those less prosperous. Those less prosperous states may view the cost of accessing the JCPC as a barrier that in effect denies access to the highest court. A complete breakdown of the GDP per capita groups at the time of independence

Table 2.1 Bivariate Probit Regression Results of Additive Indexed Variable on the Decision to Retain the JCPC

Explanatory Variable		*p-value*
Influence of the Colonial Power (U.K.)	44176 (0.1681)	0.009
Constant	5215 (0.3395)	
Psuedo R	0.1134	
Observations-squared	50	

is as follows: seven states with GDP per capita < US$1,000, thirty-two states with GDP per capita US$1,000 > US$5,000, eight states with GDP per capita $5,000 > US$10,000, and one state in each of the next three categories—GDP per capita $10,000 > US$20,000 (Trinidad and Tobago), GDP per capita $20,000 > US$30,000 (The Bahamas), and GDP per capita $30,000 > US$40,000 (Brunei).

The average GDP per capita for each state at independence is U.S. $4,197.90 (*SD* = 6042.8) and the median is U.S. $2,389. This variable controls for any comparative advantage more prosperous states may have over those less prosperous states in baring the cost of accessing the JCPC. The cost of litigant access from jurisdiction around the world was suggested as an impediment and motivation to abolish appeals to that court (Wilson 2000; Swinfen 1987; Joseph 1985). There are eighteen states with GDP per capita above the sample median of U.S. $2,389 with fifteen states (83%) that retain the JCPC at independence. Of the thirty-two states below the median GDP per capita, fifteen states (47%) retain the JCPC at independence. The descriptive analysis shows that states above the sample average have a stronger tendency to retain the JCPC than those states below the sample average. This may indicate some relationship between national wealth and retaining the JCPC. The states may associate retaining the JCPC with some continuing economic benefit to be gain from the reputation and prestige of having the JCPC as the final appellate court.

There is a control variable representing sociocultural differences reflected in the colonial society influence. A state with a larger British settler population may be more likely to identify with and share sociocultural ties with the members of the JCPC and the government of the colonial power. By the preferences afforded to British settlers in leadership positions in the colonial administration, it is assumed that they participate in and exert influence on the decision-making process with regard to drafting of the constitution leading up to independence. This influence would be commensurate with their numbers in the colony and is operationalized as the percentage of the colonial population represented by British settlers at the time of independence (Barrett 1982). This is the proxy for the strength sociocultural links between the elite and the perpetuation of colonial institutions.

The British settler population comprises an average of 6 percent (*SD* = 21.5) of the colonies at independence. The median is 0.06. Only five states (10%) have settler populations above the average of the median, and all retain the JCPC at independence. Twenty-three (51%) of the remaining forty-five states with a settler population below the average also retain the JCPC at independence. The percentage colonial populations represented by settlers from the U.K. are as follows: Settler Population: < 1 percent (forty-four states), Settler Population: > 5 percent (one state), Settler Population: > 10 percent (one state), Settler Population: > 15 percent (one state), and Settler Population: > 80 percent (three states).

The vast majority of states with settler populations below the average either abolish the JCPC at independence or soon thereafter. There are exceptions, such as Malaysia, which retained the JCPC for twenty-seven years. Also, of the thirteen Caribbean states that were former British colonies and have neither significant indigenous or settler populations, eleven (85%) retain appeals to the JCPC. This may indicate that there is some influence in states with much higher settler populations but that other factors are more significant among those states below the average settler population of 6 percent.

A colony experiencing domestic colonial conflict will influence the push for independence. A control variable for whether the colony experienced armed conflict between colonial authorities and pro-independence movements or political parties prior to being granted independence by the U.K. is necessary.

Associating the JCPC with the colonial rule they resisted, new governing coalitions may be leery of having their policies challenged before a final appellate court in the capital city of the former colonial power. Pre-independence conflict over policy preferences on the issues of governance and independence, therefore, may lead the postindependence governing coalition to reject the JCPC as a colonial institution and as being not in keeping with state sovereignty. Banks (2013) estimates the level of conflict using weighted conflict measures: assassinations, strikes, guerrilla warfare, government crises, purges, riots, revolutions, and anti-government demonstrations. For the purposes of this research, the Banks scores are represented in a binary form (1/0). Any positive Banks scores for conflict are categorized as "1" (Yes) and the absence of pre-independence conflict are categorized as "0" (No). Nine colonies experienced conflict during the five years prior to independence. Forty colonies did not experience conflict before independence while ten[12] did. Conflict with colonial authorities and institutions prior to independence may contribute to the emerging governing coalition's disenchantment with such institutions, including the JCPC. This may contribute to the apparent propensity of those colonies that experience pre-independence conflict to abolish appeals to that court at independence. Nationalist conflicts occurred in the time leading up to Nigerian independence in 1960 and Kenyan independence in 1963 (Global Literacy Project n.d.), as well as Indian independence in 1948 (Chandra, Mukherjee, Mukherjee, Panikkar, and Mahajan 2011) and Guyanese independence in 1966 (Intervention and Exploitation n.d.). The percentage of colonies experiencing armed conflict (Banks 2013) between colonial authorities and pro-independence movements or political parties prior to being granted independence is 18 percent (N = 9). Four of the nine states (46%) that experienced pre-independence conflict retained the JCPC at independence. Of the forty-one states that did not experience conflict, twenty-one states (61%) retained the JCPC at independence. When the state decides to retain the JCPC, the number of pre-independence conflicts is four (13.33%). When the state decides to abolish appeals to the JCPC, the number of pre-independence conflicts is five (25%). This shows that the number of pre-independence conflicts is not significantly higher in the states that abolish appeals to the JCPC. This is in line with the descriptive analysis of the correlation with the decision to abolish the JCPC showing weak central tendency in either the group of states that experienced conflicts to retain the JCPC or vice versa. These preliminary results suggest that pre-independence conflict does not indicate a very strong tendency to either retain or replace the JCPC. It suggests that pre-independence conflict does not influence the perception of the any benefit accrued of acceding to the JPC considering the prestige and reputation that it may afford the new state.

Finally, there is control variable for the time frame or period during which the state gained independence. The states gained independence during different periods in history since 1931. For example, the influences on state that gained independence between 1931 (Westminster Act) and 1970. This could be considered the primary period during which all European colonial powers were engaged in the decolonization process for most of the colonies in the empires. During this period, the attraction of an association with the European power may have been different as the decline in the power of the European states on the world stage (Kwon 2010) may make affiliation less attractive and beneficial. With the U.K. no longer a military and economic world power, association through membership in the British Commonwealth was probably sufficient to buttress their international credibility. The states gaining independence from 1971 to 1984 would have been received with much less international fanfare, as the states tended to be smaller. Though, the second period coincided with the process of general European decolonization that followed World War II (Fieldhouse 2011) with a plethora of new states emerging onto the world stage (Springhall 2001) the attraction of the JCPC continued through the third period which ended with Brunei gaining independence in 1984. Further, becoming a sovereign state was much more the norm, and the process routine, with the exception being Zimbabwe in 1980. In 1984, Brunei was the last colony to gain independence and retain the JCPC. An analysis of the 50 states in the following three periods identifies several states that retained the JCPC at independence: 1947 to 1970, during which 19 of the 234 new states (55%) retained the JCPC; and 1971 to 1984, during which 11 of the 16 new states (68%) retained the JCPC. During the first period (1931–1946) the tendency among the five states is to retain the JCPC. However, the subsequent periods do not reflect that tendency. In the forty-five remaining states, just over half retain the JCPC. These analyses reveal marked tendencies within the period during which the state gains independence and speaks to the influence of the perceived benefit of a perpetuating significant link with the U.K. through acceding to the JCPC at independence.

Acknowledging the limitations imposed by the relatively small number of states in the sample ($n = 50$), I estimate a multivariable probit model with the additive variable (*the length of colonial rule + type of colonial rule + the presence of a law school + whether the first prime minister was educated in the U.K.*) as a proxy for the influence of colonial rule and the five control variables. Table 2.2 presents the results of the multivariable probit model followed by a discussion and analysis of the model. The model was checked for multicollinearity[13] of the predicted variables by observing the variance inflation factor (VIF), Tolerance ($1 - R^2$), Eigenvalues, and Condition Index (CI) for each predictor in the model. If VIF values are large (greater than 10), Tolerance values are small (less than 0.1), Eigenvalues are small (close to 0), or CI is large (greater than 30), then these would be signs of multicollinearity between the covariates. None of the predictors in the models show signs of multicollinearity, as none of the VIFs values exceeded a value of four. The model tests my theory that the stronger the colonial influence, the more likely the state chooses to retain the JCPC as the final appellate court. The results show that the strength of the colonial influence is significantly associated with whether the colony abolishes appeals to the JCPC at independence ($p = 0.026$).

Table 2.2 Multivariable Probit Results of Colonial Influence on the Status of Appeals to the JCPC

Explanatory Variable		*p-value*
Colonial influence	−0.5631	0.026
	(0.2525)	
Settler population at independence	−0.5242	0.143
	(0.3574)	
GDP per capita at independence	−0.4264	0.559
	(0.7294)	
Pre-independence conflict	−0.2261	0.674
	(0.5371)	
Time frame of independence 1 (1931–1946)	2.2882	
	(2.3798)	0.336
Time frame of independence 2 (1947–1970)	0.7047	0.138
	(0.4749)	
Time frame of independence 3 (1971–1984)	0	
	(omitted)	
Constant	0.3830	0.452
	(0.5096)	
Psuedo-R-squared	0.267	
Observations	50	

This provides support for the assertion of the factor of length of colonial rule in the overall colonial influence. The longer colonial period contributes to further entrenchment of the institutions in the colonial society. The new governing coalition will be more familiar with the role of the JCPC, increasing the likelihood that it will be considered a reliable and suitable partner after independence. This colonial influence, which includes longer periods of reliance of the JCPC, serves to increase the willingness to accept this colonial institution as a reliable partner in the governing institutions of the sovereign state.

One element that may be missing from my models is a proxy for the exercise of political influence of colonial and local elites in the process by which the new constitution is written in each colony leading up to independence. This process involves the negotiations between the U.K. government and the local elite, who then lead the governing coalition into independence. Various types of commissions and committees develop as a part of that transition period from colony to independent state. In many cases, a constitutional commission serves principally in a supporting role to the legislative assembly. The primary function is to provide expert advice on constitutional problems and issues, in addition to proposing and drafting entire constitutions (Straum 1977). Commissions and the resulting constitutions are products of constraints and criteria imposed by the creators and the ultimate need for ratification by another body (Elster 1995), such as the local legislative assembly or the British parliament. Nevertheless, the process varies across the Empire. For example, before independence, the Nigeria's elected Nigerian legislature was created through the granting of internal self-government by the Lyttleton Constitution of 1954.[14] Though Nigerian nationalists were part of the process of drafting the constitution starting in 1954 and culminating with the 1958 Constitutional Conference, the legislature never ratified the Independence Constitution, nor was it referred to the Nigerian people via referendum. Instead, it was still imposed by an act of the British Parliament, and under this constitution the JCPC continued to be Nigeria's highest court (Ismail 2010). The extant literature reveals more complex constitutional deliberation over many years leading up to India's independence: The Nehru Report of 1928,[15] the Simon Commission of 1930, the Joint Committee on Indian Constitutional Reform of 1934,[16] the Supru Report[17] of 1945, the Ad Hoc Committee of the Supreme Court of 1947,[18] and culminating with the Independence Constitution of 1947 (Granville 1966). In Papua New Guinea, the domestic legislature in conjunction with the colonial authorities set the stage for transition to independence. The dominant United Party of Papua New Guinea seated seven party leaders along with four members from its ally, Pangu Pati, on the sixteen-seat Constitutional Planning Committee, which produced constitutional recommendations in the 1974 report. While the report does not provide reasons for abolishing appeals to the Privy Council, it clearly recommends that the Supreme Court be the highest court postindependence (Papua New Guinea Constitutional Planning Committee Report 1974). Lastly, the British government established the West Indian Royal Commission to examine conditions in the colonies in the Commonwealth Caribbean. This commission produced The Moyne Report in 1945. It is arguably the single most significant document in Commonwealth Caribbean history (Benn 2011) and set the stage for the individual colonies to prepare for independence. Each colony then had a domestic commission that crafted the constitution, with all thirteen colonies retaining the JCPC as the final appellate court at independence. Based on this summary review, I conclude that this would be outside the scope of this research but may be part of future research evaluating the process of developing written constitutions.

SUMMARY AND CONCLUSION

This work contributes to our understanding of the persistence of institutions or why states may accede to extraterritorial courts. The case of the British Commonwealth is used to examine why the governing coalition of a state may be influenced to continue being linked to an extraterritorial court such as the JCPC as its final appellate court. The retention of this colonial institution, seems an affront the sovereignty of the new states. The JCPC, which for all intents and purposes is a British institution, put the final adjudication of legal challenges beyond the administrative control of the governing coalition. Knowing the importance of this court, exposes why states chose the final appellant court they expected to be a reliable partner in the new governing coalition, and that each state's colonial experience influenced the decision of the new governing coalition at independence. This expectation was influenced and constrained by the influence of colonial rule. The analysis in this chapter provides support effect of the colonial experiences of each state. The results indicate that no single proxy can adequately capture the influences of history and colonial experience on the governing coalition. A multifaceted approach is used to test the theory. First, using the additive index variable, the results show that the colonial experience of the states influenced their decisions about the JCPC at independence. Cognizant of the small-n limitation on the robustness, the hypotheses are tested using multivariable probit models[19] to provide support. Model 1 shows that the additive index variable operationalizing the influence of British colonial rule is significantly associated with whether the colony retained appeals to the JCPC. Specifically, when controlling for other factors, as strength of the colonial tie increases, the less likely the colony was to abolish appeals to the JCPC at independence. This finding suggests that strength of colonial rule impacted the expectation of the emerging governing coalition that the JCPC will be a reliable partner by upholding and legitimizing its policies. Creating an additive index to capture the effects of colonial rule on the decision at independence, captures the influence of colonial rule at the first critical juncture at independence. The results of the bivariate (indicating a central tendency) and the multivariate probit model with the additive index reveal the significance of colonial rule on the decision of the governing coalition at independence. This result indicates that the place of the U.K. in the global community and its continued support for the JCPC are of some importance as part of the colonial influence. As the power of the U.K. waned after World War II (Porter 2012), it is suggested that so too did the need to be associated with the former colonial power and the prestige and reputation of the JCPC. The influence of the political environment after independence is examined in chapter 3.

Second, the Wilcoxon rank-sum tests[20] explore the individual associations of the length of colonial rule and type of colonial rule, with whether the colony retained or abolished appeals to the JCPC. Results show that when not controlling for other factors, the length of colonial rule and whether a colony experienced direct or indirect rule are individually significantly associated with whether the colony retained or abolished appeals to the JCPC. These results find support in the descriptive analysis that point to the central tendency of states that experienced colonial rule for longer than the average of 121 years for all states to retain the JCPC. Nineteen (38%) states experienced longer periods of colonial rule than the sample average, and of those nineteen states only three (16%) abolished appeals to the JCPC at independence. The analysis also indicates that states that experienced direct colonial rule tended to retain the JCPC. In 52 percent (twenty-six) of the fifty states, the percentage of total court cases following customary or traditional law was above the average of 30 percent. Of those twenty-six states, 58 percent (fifteen) of the states replaced the JCPC with a domestic final appellate court at independence.

This result provides support for the theory that characteristics and history of U.K. colonial rule significantly influences the governing coalition's view of the reliability of JCPC as a reliable partner in policy-making for furthering "peace, order and good government" (POGG) as a feature of constitutional rule (Yusuf 2014, 1). The JCPC, as an integral and important part of the British colonial governance, proved to perpetuate its association with the states despite the apparent affront to sovereignty. This exemplifies that the governing coalition is more likely to view an extraterritorial court more favorably when there is perception that the court will enhance its credibility. In other words, such an extraterritorial court would be more acceptable in the eyes of the governing coalition and would increase the likelihood that it would not be considered merely an affront to sovereignty but contribute to its legitimacy.

This research seeks to gain insight into the factors that influence the choice of court prior to independence based on factors that may influence the persistence of the relationship between states and an extraterritorial court. The case of the British Commonwealth and JCPC as an option for the final court of appeal at independence provides the states to explore a critical juncture using quantitative analyses of the factors that influence the choices of the governing coalition of the state at independence. It is at this critical juncture that the new national leadership has the first opportunity to participate in development of the new constitution, which includes the choice of final appellate court. This juncture is critical because it produces a new political and institutional equilibrium in the form of an independent state, which changes its relationship with the U.K. and other states. At independence, the constitution comes into effect, under which the new governing coalition pursues polices for POGG of the sovereign state. At this juncture states see benefits to retaining the JCPC. In the Commonwealth Caribbean all the countries retain the JCPC at independence, very few countries in Africa do so and very few in Asia/Pacific region abandon the JCPC. This variation indicates support for my theory that the colonial experience influences the decision of the new governing coalition at independence.

NOTES

1. A governing coalition coalesces from the executive, legislative, and judicial branches of government led by the governing elite. The governing elite or ruling class, which would make up the governing coalition, may include the senior political elite and bureaucrats, the leading members of the liberal professions, the growing bourgeoisie, and the leading members of the security institutions (Markovitz 1987).

2. Antigua and Barbuda, Australia, The Bahamas, Barbados, Belize, Botswana, Brunei Darussalam, Canada, Cyprus, Dominica, Fiji, The Gambia, Ghana, Grenada, Guyana, India, Jamaica, Kenya, Kiribati, Lesotho, Malawi, Malaysia, Maldives, Malta, Mauritius, Namibia, Nauru, Mozambique, New Zealand, Nigeria, Pakistan, Papua New Guinea, Rwanda, Saint Lucia, Samoa, Seychelles, Sierra Leone, Singapore, Solomon Islands, South Africa, Sri Lanka, St Kitts and Nevis, St Vincent and The Grenadines, Swaziland, Tonga, Trinidad and Tobago, Tuvalu, Uganda, United Republic of Tanzania, Vanuatu, and Zambia. Note: Bangladesh (emerged from India) and Cameroon are not former colonies.

3. Antigua and Barbuda, Bahamas, Barbados, Belize, Dominica, Grenada, Guyana, Jamaica, St. Lucia, St. Kitts and Nevis, St. Vincent and the Grenadines, and Trinidad and Tobago.

4. The first critical juncture (independence) will be different for each colony.

5. With little variation, former British colonies adopted the Westminster model of government. In reality, this model is a superimposed tailored facsimile of the British parliamentary system.

6. U.K. statute that declared the equality of Britain and the then dominions of Canada, Australia, New Zealand, South Africa, Ireland, and Newfoundland.

7. The robustness is limited by the size of the N ($n = 50$). The results are augmented with the descriptive analyses.

8. Additive index is utilized to measure "the dynamic legal forces on judicial decision" using five discrete variables to capture different aspects of each case that indicate legal certainty.

9. Customary law is used in village courts for indigenous peoples. Estimates based on the research by Ottley 2002, Brown 1999, Patterson 1995, and Zorn 1994.

10. Buddhist law: Estimate based on the research of Nyo Nyo 2005, Gutter 2001, and Kyaw 1994.

11. GDP per capita is calculated in 2012 U.S. dollars for the year of independence.

12. Botswana, Kenya, Myanmar, Zimbabwe, Cyprus, Ireland, Rep of, Nigeria, India, Malaysia, and Zambia.

13. Multicollinearity is a high degree of correlation between variables that makes it difficult to accurately decipher the effect of independent variables on dependent variables.

14. Formulated the federal principle that provided the basis for Nigeria's independence in 1960.

15. Moti Lal Nehru chaired the committee to draft a constitutional scheme for India which was delivered to a joint British and Indian leaders' conference in May 1928.

16. This committee addressed constitutional reforms for India and Burma.

17. As part of efforts to develop a constitutional scheme for Indian independence, this committee was charged with making recommendation to address issues pertaining to the contentious issues of minorities' rights and status.

18. As part of efforts to develop a constitutional scheme for Indian independence, this committee focused on fundamental constitutional rights and the federal judiciary.

19. A probit model (or *probit regression*) is a method of performing regressions for binary outcome variables. Binary outcome variables are dependent variables with two possibilities such as yes/no, positive test result/negative test result, or single/not single. A probit model estimates the probability a value will fall into one of the two possible binary outcomes of the dependent variable. Long, J. Scott. *Regression Models for Categorical and Limited Dependent Variables.* Advanced Quantitative Techniques in the Social Sciences, Number 7. Sage Publications: Thousand Oaks, CA, 1997.

20. The Wilcoxon rank-sum test is frequently used to compare of two groups of nonparametric (interval or not normally distributed) data. The groups are not measured exactly but rather as falling within certain limits specified by the researcher. Gad, S.C. Statistical Methods in Toxicology in Charlene A. McQueen (Ed.), *Comprehensive Toxicology*, accessed on June 9, 2019. https://www.sciencedirect.com/referencework/9780080468846/comprehensive-toxicology#book-info.

Chapter 3

The JCPC after Independence

INTRODUCTION

While independence from colonial rule signaled the emergence of a sovereign state, some states in every region of the British Empire retained a connection to the U.K. via the JCPC as the final appellate court. This phenomenon is observed in large Asian states such as India and Malaysia, as well as small states such as Dominica and Antigua in the Caribbean, and Kiribati and Tuvalu in the Pacific region. The phenomenon also extends to Africa where states such as The Gambia (West Africa), Kenya (East Africa), and South Africa retained the JCPC for thirty-three, three, and nineteen years, respectively. If some states retain the JCPC at independence, why may they later decide to abolish appeals to the JCPC and establish a domestic final appellate court?[1]

In effect, the states that retain appeals to the JCPC at independence perpetuate an important institutional vestige of British colonial rule. As the final appellate court, the JCPC retains the ultimate judicial power for disposing legal disputes originating in the respective state or British territory, but with the state having no input or responsibility for appointing the judges, declaring their terms of service, or funding that court (Howell 1979; Swinfen 1987). Despite its limited jurisdiction within the U.K., the JCPC is widely viewed as a "United Kingdom Institution" (Mohr 2011, 134). Defining sovereignty as having capacities or powers that can be utilized without the consent or approval of another (Brown 2002), retaining the JCPC is an apparent contradiction to modern understandings of state sovereignty and autonomy. In reality, however, thirty (60%) of the fifty states in the sample retained the JCPC at independence. Of the thirty states, seventeen states (57%) eventually abolished the right of appeal at some point before January 1, 2015. Why did these seventeen states eventually decide to abolish appeals to the JCPC?

Theorizing that, in the years postindependence, states continue to expect that the final appellate court will uphold and legitimize the policies of the governing coalition, split population survival (SPS) models[2] are used to analyze twenty-six states from Asia, Africa, and the Caribbean. The analyses start at the year of independence until the year ties are severed with the JCPC or January 1, 2015 (whichever comes first) for each state. Within the risk set of twenty-six states, 58 percent (n = 15) abolished appeals and 42 percent (n = 11) states retained appeals to the JCPC as of January 1, 2015. The purpose of this chapter is to better understand what factors after independence influenced the governing coalition to abolish appeals to the JCPC and establish a domestic final appellate court. This will provide greater insight into how states may respond to and interact with other extraterritorial courts as they emerge and develop.

After independence, the former colonies fall into three groups. First, there are those that replace the JCPC at independence with a domestic final appellate court. Second, there are those that, having retain the JCPC at independence, later decided to sever ties with it and establish their own final appellate court. Finally, some states still allow appeals to the JCPC. Of the former colonies in Group 3 that retain the JCPC at independence, some choose to form a new domestic final appellate court at another critical juncture[3] some years later. This juncture is not inevitable, but seventeen states abolished the JCPC at various times after independence. It can be argued that this second juncture (see figure 3.1) is a

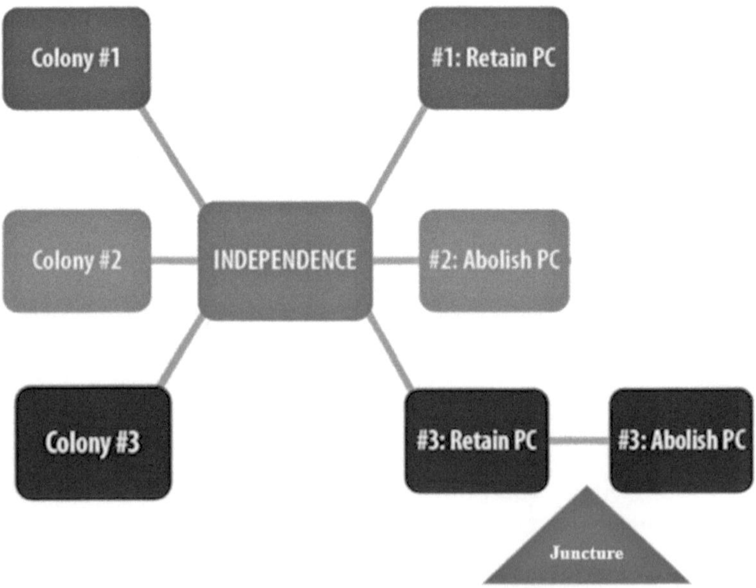

Figure 3.1 The Critical Junctures for Choosing a Final Appellate Court.

function of a changed political environment[4] and a disconnection between the policy preferences of the state and the court after independence. In other words, political changes and uncertainty as to whether the JCPC will uphold their policies may lead the governing national coalition to view the JCPC as threat to the legitimacy of their decisions (Dahl 1957) or to the new vision for the state. At the point where the governing coalition perceives this discontinuity with the JCPC as an impediment, they may move to abolish the right of appeal. It is important to better understand the factors that influence the perceptions and opinions of the governing coalition about this final appellate court as an institutional partner.

This section will discuss the second critical juncture in more detail. The closer look at the thirty states reveals a clearer picture of the realities of the postindependence political environment. At independence, former colonies fall into three categories: (a) those that abolished appeals to JCPC at independence, (b) those that retained appeals to the JCPC for a period after independence before abolishing the appeals process, and (c) those that retain appeals to the JCPC.

THEORY OF CHANGE

It can be theorized that after independence the state's governing coalition expects the final appellate court to be a reliable and significant partner in the process of policy-making. This expectation is influenced by the level of colonial influence of the U.K. on the individual state. Developments after independence, however, may influence how the governing coalitions view the continued role of the JCPC. Though not inevitable, the equilibrium established at independence may be interrupted. Changes after independence can change how the governing coalition of the state perceives the reliability of the court and ultimately the willingness to continue the relationship. The political environment could change the governing coalition's perception of the court and its sensitivity to unfavorable JCPC decisions when policies are challenged. In other words, the governing coalition may become less tolerant of decisions that do not uphold and legitimize its policies. If the governing coalition views the JCPC as less of an ally and more of an obstacle, pressure may surface for the state to sever ties with the JCPC. This is exemplified in the political debate leading up to the 1948 general elections in South Africa. While the tie to JCPC is not singled out in the literature, the entire relationship with the U.K. is intensely debated. Hyam and Henshaw (2003) note that there is a shift in the South African attitude toward political developments concerning race and racial equality in the U.K. and the Empire: "By the late 1940s many [white] South Africans recognized that British public attitudes, as well as the attitude of the British government under Labour, had become more critical of South African racial policy" (285). The Nationalist Party, with a decidedly anti-British stance and an apartheid platform, won the 1948 general elections (Hyam and Henshaw 2003). Appeals to the JCPC from South Africa were abolished in 1950, and the governing coalition quickly passed more laws entrenching racial segregation (Commonwealth Network 2015). Arguably, the new governing coalition in 1948 did not want to take the risk of successful challenges to the apartheid policies before a court in the U.K. over which it had no advantage and with which the new governing coalition perceived a disconnection.

There are two main factors that shift the governing coalition's view of the JCPC as an obstacle rather than a partner. First, a major function of a state's highest appellate court is to settle not only disputes stemming from state policy but also challenges to the legitimacy of the policies themselves. If the state believes that the final appellate court is unreliable, support for that court may erode. In the context of the JCPC, a decrease in support may lead to the eventual severance of ties and the establishment of a domestic final appellate court over which it has administrative control. Therefore, it can be hypothesized that states that receive more unfavorable decisions are more likely to cut ties with the JCPC. The decisions are observed for each state in the sample for each year from independence until the state abolishes the JCPC or January 1, 2015, whichever came first.

Second, while directly after independence most states inherited democratic structures in line with the Westminster model, the level of democratization in a state may change over time. Less democratic states, and thus more politically repressive states, will also be more suspicious of a final appellate court beyond their control. As a result, if the state becomes less democratic, the likelihood of abolishing appeals to the JCPC will increase. For example, in both Fiji and The Gambia, the military overthrew their elected governments in 1986 and 1994, respectively, resulting in an erosion of democracy and in increasingly authoritarian regimes. Further, within approximately two years of this regime change both states abolished appeals to the JCPC. These structural changes[5] to the countries' judicial systems are in part a function of them wanting to ensure that the nation's highest court is more closely allied to the governing coalition.

SECOND CRITICAL JUNCTURE: POSTINDEPENDENCE

If the JCPC remain in place at independence, another critical juncture may have surfaced some years later that led the state to abandon the JCPC and establish a domestic final appellate court. Dahl's (1957) assertion that the courts are integral to the national governing coalition makes the decision about the final court important. In the face of challenges to policies, states seek a high court that will reinforce the policies of the governing coalition. JCPC decisions that go against the state may undermine that goal. The court is, therefore, less likely to be viewed as a partner or ally. As the state has no administrative means to bring the JCPC back into line, as a U.S. president may have the opportunity to do through judicial appointments or the Congress through other administrative and jurisdictional changes, the ultimate remedy is to replace the JCPC with a national court over which some administrative leverage can be exerted. It can thus be argued that states retain the JCPC when they believe the court is likely to support the governing coalition but sever ties when they perceive the role of the JCPC as incompatible with the policies of the national governing coalition. This juncture is a function of an increasing disconnection between the policy preferences of the state and the JCPC and of a heightened sensitivity to the role of this extraterritorial court in the domestic affairs of the state. If the JCPC's decisions become increasingly unlikely to reflect the preferences of the governing coalition, this may be viewed as a threat to the legitimacy of their policy decisions (Dahl 1957). At the point where the governing coalition is convinced that this extraterritorial court threatens their policies, they may initiate the process to sever ties. This juncture is not inevitable, however, as evidenced by the fact that thirteen states retain appeals to the JCPC at the end of 2015. This chapter will now examine the factors after independence that may influence the emergence of this second critical juncture.

The divergence of preferences may prompt the governing elite to muster the political will to abolish the JCPC. After all, it is tempting for the governing coalition to assume authority over and responsibility for this important institution to increase the reliability of the entire judiciary when challenges arise. This makes unraveling the puzzle as to why states would not assume this constitutional function at independence more pressing and important. States that retain appeals to the JCPC are bound to a final appellate court that is far from the state physically, beyond the administrative control of the governing coalition, and whose judges serve on the Supreme Court of Judicature in the U.K. From the sample of fifty former colonies, thirty states (60%) that emerged from the British Empire retain the JCPC for some period after independence. Of the thirty states, seventeen eventually sever ties with the JCPC. Arguably, these thirty states are the most interesting and raise the question of why any state would change an institution it previously deemed appropriate. The extant literature does not effectively address the reasons why states that retained the JCPC as the highest appellate court would later abolish appeals to this extraterritorial court. Further, examining this phenomenon will inform our understanding of the path-dependent nature of institutional persistence. This is important as states establish and maintain ties with extraterritorial courts.

Several countries (Ghana, Guyana, India, Kenya, Nigeria, and Uganda) retain the JCPC for less than five years after independence. All these states promulgated new constitutions as part of political changes that established republics as a general attempt to further break lingering colonial influence represented by the Westminster model of government adopted at independence (Galligan and Versteeg 2013). These new constitutions also replace the JCPC with a domestic final court of appeal.

The new governing coalition in each state in this sample expects the court to be a reliable partner and legitimize their policies when challenged. This raises an important question: What postindependence changes contribute to the disconnection that leads some states to a second juncture? The reality of governing the state in a changing political environment may heighten the national coalition's sensitivity to their inability to leverage this extraterritorial court in their favor. African leaders, for example, who experienced comparatively shorter periods of colonial rule, had more limited experience governing through the "essentially alien structures hastily superimposed over the deeply ingrained political legacies of imperial rule" by the time of independence (Gordon 2007, 62). It was likely that, over time, events and changes in the political environment as well as decisions of the JCPC lead to a disconnection between the state and the JCPC. In other words, when the governing coalition perceives the JCPC as not fulfilling the role of a reliable partner, a second critical juncture may surface. At that point, it is more likely that the state will abolish the JCPC and replace it with a domestic final appellate court.

To address this second issue of why states abolish appeals to the JCPC at different times, it is theorized that after independence two factors influence whether the governing coalition continues to view the JCPC as a reliable partner in the governing coalition. The first factor includes the levels at which the JCPC uphold the policies of the governing coalition. Voigt, Ebeling, and Blume (2007) find that membership of this extraterritorial court has both a statistically and economically positive effect on economic growth, which may be attributable to the right of appeal to the JCPC and may in turn enhance the credibility of the state. The research for this chapter goes beyond Voigt, Ebeling, and Blume (2007), who only examine that affect the presence or absence of the right of appeal to the JCPC. To gain insight into the possible influence of extraterritorial court decisions on the state, this chapter will examine decisions in cases originating in states that retained appeals to the JCPC after independence and changes in the political environment. It will present a more nuanced understanding of when the state may be willing to sacrifice any perceived credibility or colonial attachment to the JCPC and move to abolish appeals by looking at JCPC cases where the state is a litigant.

It is expected that a detailed examination of JCPC decisions from each jurisdiction will reveal that a higher ratio of appeals in which the JCPC did not support the state's preference indicates a policy disconnection with the governing coalition and reinforces the notion that the court is not a reliable partner. This increases the likelihood that the state will abolish appeals to the court. It can be hypothesized (H2) that the likelihood of abolishing appeals to the extraterritorial court will increase as the state's level of success before the court decreases.

Given the role of the state is not the same in the legal challenges before the JCPC, the sensitivity and responses to the decisions may vary. The response of the state to decisions when the state is (1) the appellant; or (2) the respondent are examined. The state is the appellant in 19 percent of all the cases during the period of study. Of the twenty-six states, twenty (77%) had at least one case in which it is the appellant before the JCPC. When the lower court decision is unfavorable to the governing coalition, the onus is then on the governing coalition to utilize their resources to petition the JCPC and make the case for the appeal. Cases in which the state is the appellant before the JCPC may be particularly important. Having lost at the lower court, the state considers it important to petition the highest legal forum for relief from the decisions of the lower court. Further, losing in the domestic lower court is more publicly visible as that court is physically within the state. Unfavorable decisions may be interpreted as signaling the illegitimacy of the policy. The immediacy of this may make the governing coalition more apprehensive about responding if the reliable final appellate court is uncertain. Focusing on the JCPC's decisions in these cases may be a state barometer of court reliability. The governing coalition may be especially sensitive to the decisions of the court in these cases and may rely on the JCPC to have a legitimizing effect (Dahl 1957), having failed in the lower court. It can be hypothesized (H2.1) that the likelihood of abolishing appeals to the extraterritorial court, therefore, will increase as the state's level of success in cases where the state is the appellant decreases.

Second, changes in the political environment after independence could contribute to the second critical juncture being reached by the state. Many British colonies emerged as states with the Westminster model of government and institutions that were, in many ways, carbon copies of British constitutional practice (Juegensmeyer 1964). Changes in the political environment can evolve in different ways, with not all changes resulting in significant shifts in the status quo or in the relationship between the state and its citizens reflect in the governing institutions including the courts. These changes can disrupt the institutional equilibrium established at independence. The goal is to better understand what changes will galvanize the governing coalition to move against the JCPC. Some state leaders then change the constitution postindependence to meet the perceived needs of governing; some retain more democratic practices while other become more authoritative. A more authoritarian regime that relies less on democratic legitimacy may feel a greater need for the courts to validate their policy preferences. The literature indicates that courts in authoritarian regimes are not usually independent of the executive branch and may instead be characterized as purely an extension of administrative power for implementing ideological or political initiatives (Linz 1975; Tate and Haynie 1993). Retaining the JCPC would not conform to this characterization because the state would not have control over the court and increase the likelihood of severing ties.

Political changes could also be led by changes in the governing coalition that ushered in new visions for the state. These changes may be made via elections, as was evident in New Zealand in 1999 (Wilson 2000, 2010), or military coups, as occurred in Fiji in 1987 (Tran 2006) and The Gambia in 1994 (Jammeh 2011; Senghore 2010). Thus, the governing coalition may seek control over the final appellate court to minimize the likelihood of successful challenges to their policies and to keep the decision-making process completely within the control of the state. Some states, however, have not experienced changes in the political environment or the changes are not sufficient to influence the governing coalition's perception of the JCPC enough to take steps to abolish the court. This research will increase our understanding of how changes in the political environment influence the governing coalition's decision about continued reliance on the JCPC as the final appellate court. Therefore, states that experience political changes are more likely to abolish appeals to the extraterritorial court.

More authoritarian (less democratic) regimes also may have heightened sensitivity to the fact that the JCPC is supported and staffed in a liberal democracy and former colonial power. The perceived reliability of the JCPC in the political environment of the U.K. may be altered by the political environment of the state and the sensitivity to the courts decisions. The response to the JCPC may be a function of the heightened sensitivity cause by changes in the political environment interacting with the decisions of the court. In other words, unfavorable decisions regardless of the how many may elicit more of a reaction from the governing coalition in less democratic regimes. The decision to sever ties with the court is more likely when unfavorable decisions are handed down by the final appellate court in less democratic political environments. A less democratic political environment, therefore, heightens the governing coalition's sensitivity to unfavorable decisions resulting in an increased likelihood that appeals to the extraterritorial court will be abolished if the court hands down unfavorable decisions.

UNIT OF ANALYSIS AND SAMPLE OF STATES

While the delinking from the colonial power at independence represents the first critical juncture, the possible postindependence junction is another critical juncture. The fact that thirty of the fifty states (60%) retain the JCPC illustrates the fact that the persistence of this colonial institution in 60 percent of the states is not insignificant. The inquiry in this chapter, therefore, focuses on quantitative analysis of the factors that may influence the governing coalition to sever ties with the JCPC at some point after independence.

SPS models with time-varying covariates (TVCs) are used to conduct this analysis, with the unit of analysis being country-year ($N = 673$). The analysis examines twenty-six of the thirty states that retain the JCPC as the final appellate court for some period postindependence. The four states not included in the sample are Barbados, Belize, Kiribati, and Tuvalu. Barbados and Belize abolished appeals to the JCPC in 2010 but did not establish a domestic final appellate court. Instead, these states acceded to the CCJ established in 2001 as part of the deepening regional integration of the CARICOM (Caribbean Court of Justice 2001). While the decision of a state to trade one extraterritorial court for another is an important question in and of itself, it is outside the scope of this project. The micro-Pacific states of Kiribati and Tuvalu were also not included because there is a scarcity of consistent and reliable data on these two states.

There are twenty-six states with wide variations in the number of years the states retain the JCPC from as few as two years, in the case of Kenya, to as many as seventy-five years, in the case of New Zealand. Also, this group of states includes the eleven states that still retain the JCPC as of January 1, 2016, of which nine are in the Commonwealth Caribbean (Antigua and Barbuda, The Bahamas, Dominica, Grenada, Jamaica, St. Kitts and Nevis, St. Lucia, Trinidad and Tobago, and St. Vincent and the Grenadines) and one each in Africa (Mauritius) and Asia (Brunei). As discussed in chapter 2, these eleven states all experienced strong colonial influences as captured by the additive index scores.

This divergence may result in a reduced likelihood that the JCPC will uphold and legitimize their policies. The will to change the status quo in response to the changed view of the JCPC is influenced by the political environment, which may lead the governing national coalition to establish a domestic final appellate court. The dependent variable is therefore the state-year in which appeals to the JCPC are abolished, or the "event" occurs, in a year between 1931 and 2014. Box-Steffensmeier and Jones (2004) characterize the "event" in history analysis as "a change or transition from one state or condition of interest to another" (8). The binary dependent variable is coded for the year a state abolishes the JCPC and all other years. Based on the sample of twenty-six states, eleven states retain appeals to the JCPC as of January 2015 and the fifteen states that abolished appeals at some point before January 1, 2015.

Changes in those influences can be significant enough to cause the governing coalition to change the status quo after independence and replace the JCPC with a domestic final appellate court. The choice of the state at this second critical juncture is underpinned by whether the governing coalition perceives the JCPC as a reliable partner in policy-making. Each state's political environment with six independent variables comprises four primary explanatory variables and two control variables are operationalized. The next section presents how the variables are measured with some descriptive analyses that provide useful information on tendencies and patterns (Laerd Statistics 2013) to aid the analyses using the six SPS models. Table 3.1 presents the summary statistics for all the variables of interest used in testing the postulates.

The first primary explanatory variable is the percentage of all cases before the JCPC in each year won by the state where the state is a party (respondent or appellant). Analyzing the state-year reveals the level of success the states had in actual cases. All cases adjudicated by the JCPC are available online through the British and Irish Legal Information Institute (2014). From the universe of cases adjudicated by the JCPC, this chapter is interested in all the cases where the state is a party. This represents a broad spectrum of cases involving legal challenges to the policies of the governing coalition on appeal to the JCPC as the final appellate court. Table 3.2 displays the decisions

Table 3.1 Summary Statistics: The Independent and Control Variables

Variable	*Obs.*	*Mean*	*Std. Dev.*	*Min.*	*Max.*
State Win Ratio in all cases	673	0.78	0.36	0	1
State Win Ratio when state is the appellate (salient)	673	0.88	0.31	0	1
State Win Ratio when state is the respondent	673	0.81	0.34	0	1
State conflict	640	224.08	704.90	0	6312
State GDP per capita	673	6448.71	3803.20	617	21314
Democratization	N	%			
Free	568	85.80			
Partially Free	62	9.37			
Not Free	32	4.83			

Table 3.2 JCPC Decisions Disaggregated by a Total in Each of the Following Categories of Law: (1) Constitutional Rights, (2) Torts/Administrative Law, (3) Criminal Law, and (4) "Other Areas" of Law

Category of Law	*Number of Cases*
Constitutional/Individual rights	225
Tort/Administrative law	168
Criminal law	330
Others areas of law	142
Total	856

disaggregated by a total in each of the following categories of cases: (1) constitutional rights, (2) torts/administrative law, (3) criminal law, and (4) "other areas" of law where the state is a party.

These cases are reviewed for each state-year between the date of independence and removal of the JCPC or January 1, 2015. The win-rate is calculated based on the total number of cases in each year from 0 to 100 percent. The years in which there are no cases are coded as the state being 100 percent successful. There are of 864 cases originating from the twenty-six states between the date of independence and removal of the JCPC or January 1, 2015, whichever came first.

To get a more nuanced picture of state success rates before the JCPC, the average favorable decisions in each state-year are disaggregated by decisions where the state is the respondent (second explanatory variable) and those where the state is the appellant (third explanatory variable). This may provide more insight into whether the governing coalition is more sensitive when it must respond to a challenge in the final appellate court or when the state is not satisfied with the decision of the lower court and decides to take the case to the final court of appeal. In the latter situation, the state decides that they are significant enough to invest public resources to appeal the decision of the lower domestic court. In these cases, the governing coalition would like to be able to rely on the JCPC to uphold and legitimatize its policies. It is almost impossible to say with certainty that any single unfavorable decision leads the governing coalition directly to the decision to replace the JCPC. Mohr (2011) asserts, however, that such decisions sharpen calls for reforming or abolishing appeals to the JCPC:

> Examples of decisions of this nature include *Webb v. Outrim* in Australia; *Nadan v. R* in Canada; *Pearl Assurance Co. Ltd. v. Government of the Union* in South Africa; *Wigg and Cochrane v. Attorney General* in the Irish Free State; *Lesa v. Attorney General in New Zealand* and *Pratt and Morgan v. AG of Jamaica* in the Caribbean. (135)

Other specific examples are worth noting and provide some indication of the importance of the JCPC's decision. In 1971, the year before Sri Lanka abolished appeals to the JCPC, three cases are decided, and the state prevails in only one (33 percent). In one case (*The Commissioner of Inland Revenue of Columbo v J. M. Rajaratnam*[6]) where the state is the appellate, the JCPC decision is not in favor the state. In Canada, the JCPC hands down unfavorable decisions in the last two cases in which the state was the appellant. Similarly, in Malaysia, in the last five cases before Malaysia abolishes appeals to the JCPC, there are only two decisions favorable to the state. This might indicate that the state views the unfavorable decisions as an indication of a disconnection with the JCPC.

The fourth explanatory variable is regime type postindependence. The level of democracy has shown to influence the likelihood of political repression (Davenport 1998) with the potential to curb the possible abusive behavior of political leadership through judicial and legislative restraints (Keith and Ogundele 2007). The type of regime may vary over time after independence on a democratic-autocratic regime spectrum. This independent variable is employed in the models to tests whether as a regime becomes less democratic over time, the likelihood of the governing coalition abolishing appeals to the JCPC increases. De Bruijn (2014) points out that no single measure "can objectively capture the full range of measurements for a stable, free, and democratic governed country" (9). To improve the operationalization of this variable, two data sources, (1) Polity IV (2013) and (2) Freedom House (2014a) are used. First, the Polity IV indicator of regime type is based on the Eckstein and Gurr (1975) design. Polity IV produces a single score for each state in each year which ranges from +10 (full democracy) to −10 (full autocracy). The limitation of only relying on this indicator is that states with populations below 500,000 are not included. Of the twenty-six states in the risk set, eight (Antigua and Barbuda, The Bahamas, Brunei, Dominica, Grenada, St. Kitts and Nevis, St. Lucia, and St. Vincent and the Grenadines) are not included in the Polity IV (2013) project. Second, Freedom House (2014) country ratings assess states on both "Political Rights" and "Civil Liberties." Both are measured on a one-to-seven scale, with one scored as most free and seven the least. The issue, however, is that Freedom House scores begin in 1972, excluding the periods of interest for three states: Canada (1931–1949), South Africa (1931–1950), and Sri Lanka (1949–1972). Guided by previous work on bilateral trade by de Bruijn (2014), a new regime type score that utilizes scores from Polity IV Project (2013) and Freedom House (2014) was created in order to solve data limitations with each existing measure. A "new score" called *Democratization* was developed by mapping the Polity IV scores with those from Freedom House for each year of available data and assigning a value. Assessments determined how each defines its categories, the differences between each, and how changes in the category contribute to the change in score. Those states

Table 3.3 Polity IV and Freedom House Scores Mapped to the Democratization Score

	Polity IV Score (−10 to 10)	*Freedom House Score (1 to 7)*	*Democratization Score (1, 0, −1)*
Not Free/More Autocratic	−10 → −4	7 → 6	−1
Partially Free/Incoherent	−3 → 3	5 → 4	0
Free/More Democratic	4 → 10	3 → 1	1

with a Polity IV rating from 10 to 4 and Freedom House score from 1 to 3 are scored "1" for Free/More Democratic; a Polity IV rating from 3 to - 3 and Freedom House score from 4 to 5 are scored "0" for Partially Free/Incoherent; and a Polity IV rating from - 4 to - 10 and Freedom House score from 6 to 8 are scored a "-1" for Not Free/More Autocratic. Table 3.3 displays how the scores from Polity IV and Freedom House are mapped to produce the new score assigned for each category of the *Democratization Score*.

To place a state in a specific category, the state's first *Democratization Score* is compared with the score for the year immediately before the year the state abolishes the JCPC or January 1, 2015, whichever comes first. Of the three states that, over time, become more democratic, two (66%) still retain the JCPC. For example, Sri Lanka is one state that becomes more democratic yet abolishes the JCPC. Ten of the thirteen (76%) states that exhibit no change still retain the JCPC. The three states with no change—Australia, Canada, and New Zealand—eventually abolish the JCPC. Nine of the ten (90%) states that can be broadly categorized as more autocratic abolish appeals to the JCPC. The only state that is less democratic at the end of the research period that retains the JCPC is Jamaica.

The results indicate the tendency of less democratic states to replace the JCPC, as opposed to those states that become more democratic or remain the same. Since there are states that do abolish the JCPC even though they become more democratic or exhibit no change in the regime, there may be something else occurring in the political environment that is not captured by using the Polity IV and Freedom House scores.

Two control variables are utilized. The first control variable is the level of conflict in each state in each year of analysis. Conflict within the state may influence the governing coalition's perception of how to maintain POGG and the extent to which it needs to exercise control over the judiciary as a part of the governing institutions. The existence and level of conflict is operationalized using DataBanks (2015a, 2015b). This database uses a weighted domestic conflict score that reflects a weighted count of incidents as conflicts. The following incidents of conflict are included in the score: (1) assassinations, (2) strikes, (3) guerrilla warfare, (4) government crises, (5) purges, (6) riots, (7) revolutions, and (8) anti-government demonstrations. Scores range from 0 to a maximum of 6250 in a country-year for the sample states.

Second, a control variable for each state's GDP per capita per country-year is included. This is a proxy for the fiscal capacity of the government and private litigants to afford pursuing cases before the JCPC in London. Appeals to the JCPC are often critiqued as "a rich man's appeal" (Mohr 2011, 132). Litigants incur added costs and inconvenience to access the JCPC (Swinfen 1987). Wilson (2000) points out that some litigants cannot afford to pursue their case at the JCPC, effectively denying them their full rights of appeal. Less prosperous states may therefore view the costs associated with accessing the JCPC as a barrier that effectively denies access to justice. Therefore, control for each state's wealth examines the comparative advantage more prosperous states may have over those less prosperous states, measured as the GDP per capita of each state in each year the state appears in the data. The estimate of the GDP for each state is in U.S. dollars, as valued in 1990 International Geary-Khamis dollars (The Maddison-Project 2013). This method is "the most widely used aggregation method for multilateral comparison of prices and real product" using "purchasing power parities of currencies and average prices of commodities" (Rao and Selvanathan 1990, 5). The growth in GDP per capita of states varies widely. For example, The Gambia's GDP per capita only increased from US$846 at independence in 1965 to US$851 in 1998 when that state abolished appeals to the JCPC. New Zealand's GDP per capita, on the other hand, increased from US$4,475 in 1931 to US$18,231 in 2005 when that state abolished all appeals to the JCPC (The Maddison-Project 2013). The average GDP per capita for all states during the period of analysis is US$6448.71. A snapshot of the fifteen states the year before they abolish the JCPC shows that four (27%) states are above the average. Of the eleven states that retain the JCPC, ten (91%) are above the average. This may indicate a tendency of states with fewer resources to abolish the JCPC and, conversely, those with higher GDP per capita to retain. GDP per capita, however, is a rather "blunt" instrument as it does not capture the resources of those in the economic elite (but not part of the governing coalition) who may be more likely to challenge the state and want to pursue an appeal to the JCPC. Further, four (Australia, Canada, New Zealand, and Singapore) of the fifteen states that abolish the JCPC are among the richest states in the world (The World Bank 2017).

EXPLORING CHANGES AFTER INDEPENDENCE

After independence, eleven states in the sample of twenty-six states do not abolish the JCPC by the end of the research period (January 1, 2015), while fifteen states do in some year prior to 2014. With no states that experience the event, it is appropriate to use a "split population" model design. The "spsurv"[7] STATA[8] command developed by Jenkins (2001), discrete time SPS modeling, and TVCs were utilized to test the above hypotheses about the decision of a state to eventually sever ties with the JCPC postindependence. This approach jointly estimates the hazard rate of both groups of states. The objective is to analyze when the event or "failure" (abolishing appeals to the JCPC) occurs and what factor contributes to our understanding of what influences the event (Bartels 2003; Fenno 1986). Assuming that the occurrence of the event or failure is not a function of time and the event does not occur in some states, this nonparametric model is preferred.

As a partial likelihood model, the SPS model assumes that there is no information regarding the relationship between covariates and the hazard rate being gleaned from the intervals between successive events (Collet 1994). This is as result of not being directly parameterized with a baseline function or intercept. The benefit of this approach is that it makes better use of available data by ordering events. The start of the analysis is left-truncated at the date of independence for each country. Further, at any time all cases are at risk of failing and the risk set decreases by one, successively dwindling as events occur. The coefficients are parameterized in terms of the hazard rate, so a positive coefficient indicates that the hazard is increasing as a function of the covariate (Box-Steffensmeier and Jones 2004).

While parametric models such as the Weibull, exponential, and Gomertz explicitly account for the "duration dependence or the extent to which the risk of experiencing the event increases or decreases as a function of time . . . , non-parametric models leave the baseline unspecified or unconstrained as to a specific distribution form" (Bartels 2003, 1). In line with Box-Steffensmeier and Zorn (2001; see also Box-Steffensmeier and Jones 2004), the theory does not allow the specification of a probability distribution for the time until the event occurs. In such cases, the absence of the need to parameterize time dependency is an advantage. Further, these SPS models effectively relax the baseline assumption by "splitting" the observations based on time intervals during the period of analysis with no assumption that the event will occur (Schmidt and Witte 1989).

RESULTS

As exemplified by every region of the Commonwealth, some states that retain appeals to the JCPC at independence later decide to abandon that extraterritorial court and establish a domestic final appellate court. Based on the sample of twenty-six states, fifteen states abolish appeals at some point after independence and eleven states retain appeals to the JCPC as of January 1, 2017. The decision to replace the JCPC is more likely if the governing coalition perceives a disconnection between the decisions of the JCPC and the state's policies. The perceived divergence may result in a reduced likelihood that the JCPC will uphold and legitimize their policies. Further, the expectation that the JCPC will be a reliable partner may be altered in the context of the changing political environment, prompting the governing coalition to take steps to abolish that right of appeal and establish a domestic final appellate court.

The dependent variable is the state-year in which appeals to the JCPC are abolished, or the "event" occurs, in a year between 1931 and the end of 2014. The Kaplan-Meier graph captures the change in the portion of states that abolish the JCPC over time, and at the same time includes those states that do not abolish the JCPC by the end of the period of analysis. Plotting the estimated survival probabilities (vertical axis) over the time of the analysis produces a survival curve that is displayed as a step function (Goel, Khanna, and Kishore 2010). The intervals indicate that a state abolishes the JCPC (occurrence of the event), and the change on the vertical axis (0, 1) indicates the change in the cumulative probability as time passes (Rich et al. 2010). Figure 3.2 displays the Kaplan-Meier Survival Estimates by whether the state retained (occurrence = 0) or abolished the JCPC (occurrence = 1). For the states that abolish the JCPC, the cumulative probability is greatest in the first thirty years of the period of analysis and more states abolish the JCPC during that period.

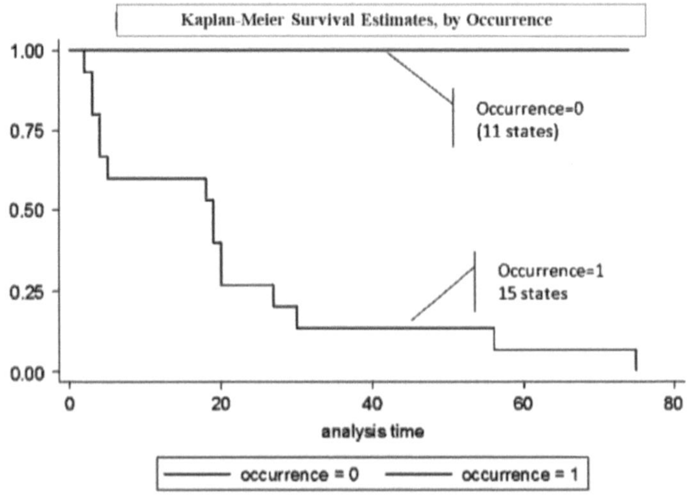

Figure 3.2 Kaplan-Meier Survival Estimates by whether the State Retained or Abolished Appeals to the JCPC.

As described in detail in chapter 1, a state's governing coalition expects the final appellate court to support their policies. In this case, it is asserted that the decision of whether to abolish appeals to the JCPC is influenced by the decisions of that court and the temporal political environment. With the independent variables described, five SPS models are estimated to examine the relationship between the state's decisions to abolish appeals to the JCPC and the decisions of that court and the political environment of the sample states. In the first model, the following is regressed: (1) the measure of the state's win ratios in all JCPC decisions decided from each country-year, (2) the dichotomous dependent variable for whether the JCPC is abolished, and (3) the control variables described earlier. In the second model, the variable values for the state win averages when the state is the respondent are employed. In the third model, the variable values when the state is the respondent and the win averages when the state is the appellant, respectively. In Model 4, both the win average when the state is the respondent and when the state is the appellant are regressed. Finally, Model 5 examines the effect of the interactive variable—values for the nature of the regimes over time and the win average in all decisions. The same control variables are included in each model.

Model 1, tests Hypothesis 2 that the lower the state's win average in JCPC decisions, the more likely the governing coalition's decision to abolish appeals to the JCPC. The results in Model 1 (Table 3.4) show that the percentage of JCPC decisions that favor the state in all decisions while controlling for intrastate conflict and GDP per capita is not significantly associated with the governing coalition's decision to abolish appeals to the JCPC. This

Table 3.4 Split Population Survival Models 1 and 2

Explanatory Variables	*Model 1*	*p-value*	*Model 2*	*p-value*
State Win Average in all Decisions	−0.785 (0.621)	0.206		
State Win Average when State is the Appellant			−1.235 (0.587)	0.035
Democratization Score	−1.462 (0.437)	0.001	−1.445 (0.435)	0.001
State Conflict	0.0001 (0.0003)	0.813	0.00003 (0.0003)	0.916
State GDP per capita	0.0003 (0.00008)	0.714	0.00003 (0.00008)	0.750
Constant	−1.918 (.622)	0.002	−1.531 (0.04)	0.013
Cure Probability	0.11003 (0.1011)	0.043	0.108224 (0.1002)	0.042
ChiSq (df)	11.32	0.045	13.63	0.0181
Observations	673		673	

result suggests that states are not responding to their relative success rates (including the years when there were no JCPC decisions). The governing coalition may not have considered the years in which there were no JCPC decisions as a "success" or "win." It may simply be that the status quo was maintained because the JCPC failed to attract their attention in those years and may not reflect any level of satisfaction with the JCPC. The null hypothesis is therefore not rejected for Hypothesis 2. The absence of any significance of the overall success of the state may suggest that the governing coalition is driven by a more discerning approach to the JCPC decisions. While all cases to which the state is a party involve some aspect of policy, unfavorable decisions may not always galvanize the political will to act. The governing coalitions generally may not perceive all unfavorable decisions as significant enough to pass a constitutional amendment to abolish appeals to the JCPC. To further examine the cases, the sample of cases are disaggregated into those where the state is the respondent and those in which the state is the appellate before the JCPC.

Model 2 tests Hypothesis 2.1 that the lower percentages of favorable JCPC decisions when the state was the appellate increase the likelihood that the governing coalition will move to abolish appeals to the JCPC. The result in Table 3.4 shows that the percentage of favorable JCPC decisions when the state was the appellant is significant ($\beta = -1.235$, *p-value* = 0.035), with the coefficient indicating the influence is in the predicted direction. To help with the interpretation of the coefficient, it is best to convert the coefficient to a hazard ratio by using exponentiation (Exp). The coefficient corresponds to a hazard ratio of 0.29 (Exp $(-1.235) = 0.29$), implying that for every unit increase in the success ratio of cases where the state is the appellant, there is a 71 percent lower chance of abolishing appeals to the JCPC, while controlling for other factors in the model. The null hypothesis may be rejected for Hypothesis 2.1.

Based on the disaggregation of the variable for the state win average in all decisions, the effect of the win average in decisions when the state was the respondent are explored further. The win average when the state was the respondent is not significant in Model 3 (Table 3.5). Considering the results from the Models 1 through 3, where the success rate of the state is only significant when the state is the appellant, this may indicate that the governing coalitions are not closely monitoring their success rate in all cases over time before the court. This is an important finding and one is returned to in chapter 5 when looking at cases and the political environment in three specific states.

Keeping in mind the theory that the governing coalition is influenced by level of state favorable decisions handed down by the JCPC and the political environment, this chapter interacts the proxies for these two variables. The changes in the political environment make it more likely that the governing

Table 3.5 Split Population Survival Models 3 and 4

Explanatory Variables	*Model 3*	*p-Value*	*Model 4*	*p-value*
State Win Average when State is the Respondent	−0.9859 (0.630)	0.118	−0.6775 (0.6807)	0.320
State Win Average when State is the Appellant			−1.0437 (0.6181)	0.091
Democratization Score	−1.5232 (0.00008)	<0.0001	−1.4769 (0.4334)	0.001
State Conflict	0.00004 (0.0003)	0.782	0.00004 (0.0003)	0.894
State GDP per capita	−0.00003 (0.00008)	0.682	−0.00004 (0.00007)	0.651
Constant	−1.6755 (0.6758)	0.013	−1.0902 (0.7557)	0.149
Cure Probability	0.11368 (0.1031)	0.045	0.11091 (0.1020)	0.044
ChiSq (df)	11.98	0.035	14.55	0.024
Observations	673		673	

coalition will responded to lower levels of favorable decisions by the court. The goal is to gain more insight into the interactive effect of these variables, where the influence of each may be more difficult to determine independently. Model 5 includes the interactive variable *Win Rate Environment* (*Win_Ratio* Democratization Score*). The analysis results employing this new variable, *Win Rate Environment*, and the control variables are displayed in Table 3.6. The *Win Rate Environment* is approaching significance ($\beta = 0.01449$, Exp (β) = 1.01, *p-value* = 0.059). Specifically, for every one unit increase in the *Win Rate Environment*, there is a 1 percent higher hazard of abolishing appeals

Table 3.6 Split Population Survival Model 5

Explanatory Variables	*Model 5*	*p-value*
Win Rate Environment (*State Win Average in all Decisions* Democratization Score*)	0.01449 (0.0077)	0.059
State Win Average in all Decisions	−0.0159 (0.0065)	0.015
State Win Average when State is the Appellant Democratization Score	−1.9649 (0.6289)	0.002
State Conflict	0.00022 (0.0003)	0.418
State GDP per capita	−0.00003 (0.00008)	0.750
Constant	−1.9613 (0.6075)	0.001
ChiSq (df)	13.90	0.031
Observations	673	

to the JCPC, while controlling for other factors in the model. This may be an indication that the political environment has heightened sensitivity of the governing coalition to the decisions of the court.

The effect of the multiplicative terms (*Win_Ratio* Democratization Score*) shows the conditional relationship of each variable when the other is held at "0" (Judd, McClellard, and Ryan 2009; Williams 2015). In partially free states (i.e., when *Democratization Score* is held at 0), a one standard deviation decreases in the level of the regime in terms of democratic scores increase the relative risk that the governing coalition will remove the JCPC by 86 percent ($\beta = 1.9649$, Exp (β) = 0.14, *p-value* = 0.002). Result shows a significant interaction effect between *Win_Ratio* and *Democratization Score* ($\beta = 0.01449$, Exp (β) = 1.0146, *p-value* = 0.059) at a 94 percent confidence level.

A significant interaction suggests that the relationship between *Democratization Score* and the hazard of abolishing appeals to the JCPC, changes by *Win_Ratio values*. Specifically, the marginal effect of the *Democratization Score* on the hazard of abolishing appeals to the JCPC where the relationship between the *Democratization Score* and the hazard of abolishing appeals to the JCPC can be seen increasing as *Win_Ratio* values also increase. In other words, the effect of *Democratization Scores* on the hazard of abolishing appeals to the JCPC increases as the *Win_Ratio* values increase. For example, it shows that when win ratio = 0, the effect of democratization score is −1.96. A1-point increase in democracy increases the log-odds of the event by −1.96). On the other hand, when win ratio = 1, the effect of democracy is −1.95, so a 1-unit increase in the level of democracy decreases the log-odds of the event by −1.95 (instead of −1.96).

Now the marginal effect of the state winning of appeal before the JCPC will be examined. The marginal effect of win ratio as the democratization score changes. When the state win ratio in all cases is at 0 percent (i.e., when *Win_Ratio* is held at 0), a one standard deviation decrease in the success rate of the state in all decisions increases the likelihood of the governing coalition removing the JCPC by 2 percent ($\beta = -0.0159$, Exp (β) = 0.98, *p-value* = 0.015). The interaction effect itself is rather small here, as the coefficient is little changed regardless of the value of win ratio. Considering the lack of significance of the state's overall level of success in the court's decision as displayed in Model 1, the finding of a marginal effect in the interaction with the political environment is worthy of note. It provides some support for the theory that the political environment does influence how the decisions of the court are viewed and ultimately whether the court itself is perceived as a reliable partner for the governing coalition. Ultimately, the unfavorable decisions of the court are viewed differently when the political environment becomes less democratic.

The variable *Democratization* is significant in all models. There is, therefore, strong support for Hypothesis 3 that the nature of the regime postindependence may underpin the political environment in which it was more likely that the governing coalition would abolish appeals to the JCPC. The results suggest that a decrease in the level of democracy, or increase in autocracy, increases the chances that the court will be abolished. In other words, decreased levels of democracy have a significant negative influence on how the governing coalition views the presence of the JCPC and the options available to those challenging their policies to appeal to this extraterritorial court that is beyond their administrative control. Finally, the results for the control variables (*State Conflict* and *GDP per capita*) are consistently insignificant across all models. The results adhere to expectations and the null hypothesis can be rejected.

The results provide support for the theory that the governing coalitions in more authoritarian regimes seem more sensitive to the presence of JCPC as an extraterritorial court over which they have no control. The governing coalitions in more authoritarian regimes are less likely to want to respond to challenges to their policies before such a court. Continuing appeals to such a court risks not having policies upheld and legitimized. The fact that the results show that the level of success in all cases is not significant leads me to conclude that the governing coalition is more concerned when they feel they must appeal to the JCPC. In these cases, they are being forced to challenge the decision of a lower court that was not in their favor. Another factor could be that more democratic states are less likely to advance policies that get challenged in court and are less sensitive to the risk of an unfavorable decision when a legal challenge is launched. For example, Singapore is classified as "partially free" by Freedom House (2015). Of the twenty cases in which the state is a litigant, three cases involve state action against opposition leaders. This may indicate some sensitivity to specific types of cases. Of the 112 cases in New Zealand, which is always classified as "free," none of the cases involve state action against opposition politicians.

SUMMARY AND CONCLUSION

The goal of this chapter is to provide insight into the factors that influence whether the state's governing coalition will change the final appellate court. The results of the SPS analysis on the twenty-six states in the sample that retain the JCPC at independence are based on the theory that the new governing coalition in each state expects the court to be a reliable partner and legitimize their policies when challenged. Decisions of the JCPC and changes in the political environment on a democratic-autocratic continuum are examined. Little support is found for the significance of the overall success of the governing coalition in JCPC decisions and strong support is found for the effect of changes in the political environment over time after independence. The models generally perform in the fashion expected, considering the theory and the consequent hypotheses. The results generally support the two tenets of this theory. First, that governing coalitions are somewhat responsive to decisions of the JCPC. More specifically, unfavorable decisions when the state is the appellant increases the likelihood the JCPC will be replaced. Second, that the governing coalition's perceptions about that court are influenced by changes in the political environment. These changes may serve to heighten the sensitivity of the governing coalition to court decisions and influence the governing coalition to abolish appeals to the JCPC. However, the evidence is not particularly strong and points to the need to examine the decisions more closely.

These findings have important implications for the long-term support and development of new extraterritorial courts. States may be leery of acceding to extraterritorial courts if the perception is that the court will not support its policies. The state will be particularly concerned about how the court is formulated and administered. Understanding the control that it has over domestic courts and its benefits, a court that is not within the control of the governing coalition control may be suspect. Further, if a state does accede then the results indicate that the state will ultimately abandon the court if the court hands down unfavorable decisions, particularly if the case is important to domestic legitimacy and the reputation of the governing coalition. Yet the response to the court is dependent of the domestic political environment. Changes in the governing coalition and political environment may also influence any ongoing commitment to the court. Depending on the judicial branch to uphold and legitimize its policies, domestic access to an extraterritorial court may be viewed with suspicion and the level of tolerance may be lower in less democratic regimes. Ultimately, therefore, the level of skepticism to utilize or willingness to tolerate unfavorable decisions will influence the longevity and vitality of an extraterritorial court.

Further, what these quantitative analyses do not capture is whether changes in governing regimes in democratic states may change the perception of and willingness to continue supporting an extraterritorial court. Tate and Hanie (1993) point out the tendency of autocratic regimes not to favor independent judiciaries. The examination of the sample shows, however, that even strongly democratic regimes such as New Zealand and Australia eventually abandon the JCPC despite its stellar reputation and independence. Further, the recent South African response to the ICC and the U.K.'s threat to withdraw from the ECJ also are informative. This raises an important question of whether other changes in the political environment or institutional structures not captured in this chapter's quantitative analyses could lead the governing coalition to abandon an extraterritorial court such as the ECJ, International Criminal Court, or the Inter-American Commission on Human Rights (ICAHR). Research suggests, however, that the state is concerned with the perceived reliability of the extraterritorial court which in turn is influenced by the political environment.

Based on this, the development of the CCJ is examined as a part of regional integration of the Commonwealth Caribbean. The CCJ presents another alternative to the JCPC or establishing a domestic final court of appeal in each state. The CCJ is reminiscent of the ECJ but significant institutional differences and is exemplary of a regional extraterritorial court outside of the EU.

NOTES

1. A domestic final appellate court is the highest level of appeal within a jurisdiction. Decision of this court are final law unless the legislature change the relevant statute or amends the constitution.
2. SPS models (spsurv) assume that a proportion of the sample (N) never fail and estimates this proportion together with the parameters characterizing the hazard rate for the remainder of the population (Jenkins 2001).
3. A critical juncture is a point when a specific choice is made among two or more options. Mahoney (2000).
4. In this work, political environment is defined as a collection of factors characterizing the political and institutional relationships between the government and the people. This is influenced by the ideology and activities of the party in power and authoritarian rule via single party rule or dictatorship (military or civilian).
5. In this work, structural changes are amendments to laws and constitutions that change political and institutional relationships between the government and the people.
6. *The Commissioner of Inland Revenue of Columbo v J. M. Rajaratnam*, 38 UKPC (1971).
7. Ibid., note 2.
8. STATA is a powerful statistical software that enables users to analyze, manage, and produce graphical visualizations of data. It is primarily used by researchers in the fields of economics, biomedicine, and political science to examine data patterns. Stata: Data Analysis and Statistical Software: Getting Started with Stata (August 2018).

Chapter 4

The Rise of the Caribbean Court of Justice (CCJ)

INTRODUCTION

An important postcolonial bond between the former British colonies and the U.K. is JCPC. The JCPC serves as a final court of appeal for colonies and former colonies who wish to retain this constitutional and legal link to the U.K. after independence. While all twelve former British colonies in the West Indies retained the JCPC at independence, it remains the final court of appeal for eight of the twelve. The four states that have acceded to the CCJ are Barbados, Belize, Guyana, and Dominica.

To better understand the emergence of the CCJ, it important to clarify the general term "the Caribbean" for the purposes of this work. The term depends greatly on standpoint and background (Girvan 2001). Terms such as Caribbean Basin or Wider Caribbean are common and can include countries such as Cuba and the Dominican Republic that are former Spanish colonies. The CCJ, however, emerged from former British Caribbean colonies sharing "language and identity, geography, history and culture, geopolitical, geo-economics, or organization" (Garvin 2001, 4). This is based on the culmination of a shared British colonial past. These states experienced a median of 207.5 years of British colonial rule (mean 223.5 years) compared to a median of 77 years (mean 93 years) for all other states in the British Commonwealth (median 87 years and average of 120.9 years). Primarily, however, this chapter utilizes the regional organization called the CARICOM which is originally all the Anglophone states. It now, however, includes Suriname (former Dutch colony) and Haiti (former French colony). The Anglophone states of CARICOM are also members of the British Commonwealth that includes most former British colonies.

During the decolonization process after World War II, the short-lived West Indies Federation (1958–1962) was the first effort at integrating the Anglophone Caribbean's emerging states—Antigua and Barbuda, Barbados, Dominica, Grenada, Jamaica, Montserrat, the then St Kitts-Nevis-Anguilla, St. Lucia, St. Vincent, and Trinidad and Tobago (CARICOM 2001). A new initiative starting in 1965 with the Agreement of Dickenson Bay[1] (Antigua and Barbuda, Barbados and Guyana) led to establish the CARIFTA in 1971 (Yankana 2006; Andic, Andic, and Dosser 2011). CARIFTA include Antigua and Barbuda, Barbados, Guyana, Trinidad and Tobago, Dominica, Grenada, St. Kitts and Nevis, St. Lucia, St. Vincent and the Grenadines, Jamaica, Montserrat, and Belize. This was replaced by the Treaty of Chaguaramas[2] in 1973 which established the CARICOM. This was revised in 2002 to facilitate the establishment of a single market and economy (CARICOM 2018). The creation of the CCJ is officially provided in Article 172 Section 8 the revised treaty in 2001 (Revised Treaty of Chaguaramas Establishing the CARICOM Including the CARICOM Single Market and Economy 2001). Based in Trinidad and Tobago, the CCJ was created in 2005 with four (Barbados, Belize, Dominica, and Guyana) members as of January 1, 2018.

The next section will discuss the JCPC in more detail and its links to the legal systems of the Commonwealth Caribbean states.

THE ROLE OF THE JCPC

The JCPC is a supranational court that hears appeals for criminal and civil cases arising from every colony and overseas territory ruled by the U.K. (Howell 1979; Swinfen 1987). The Law Lords are appointed for life by the monarch, based on nominations by the prime minister, with the advice of the Lord Chancellor who is the Speaker of the House of Lords (Malleson 1999) and the U.K.'s chief judicial officer and member of the cabinet. The colonies had no fiscal responsibility for or control over the Privy Council or appointments to the court. Interestingly, however, several former colonies retained the Privy Council as their highest national court postindependence. Thus, even though these former colonies declared their sovereignty, established separate legal and political systems, and exercised control within their own borders, many of them also decided to allow the Privy Council to continue exercising final decision-making power in domestic cases. With the authority to uphold, vary, or overrule decisions, the Privy Council is the final legal authority in these now-sovereign countries.

The former disconnects the colonies from the colonial power and is not a recent or unique observation. Burnham (2005) cites the still relevant words of Lord Brougham uttered in 1828:

> It is obvious that, from the mere distance of those colonies and the immense variety of matters arising in them, foreign to our habits and beyond the scope of our knowledge, any judicial tribunal in this country [the U.K.] must of necessity be an extremely inadequate court of review. (171)

The quality of the JCPC decisions is an important part of its credibility and the high quality of the Law Lords is not seriously questioned in the literature. Some of their decisions, however, are vigorously debated. New states, having not established an independent reputation for impartial adjudication, perceive a benefit from the right to appeal to the JCPC as it increases the credibility of their policy preferences (Voigt, Ebeling, and Blume 2007). Where the goal of the state is to induce growth, research indicates that simply promising an independent judiciary is not sufficient to induce growth (Feld and Voigt 2003). The final court, appellate court, confers legitimacy on (a) the policies of the dominant majority and (b) the basic patterns of behavior required for the operation of a democracy (Dahl 1957). Whittington (2007) reframes Dahl's position on the U.S. Supreme Court as being friendly or sympathetic to the dominant majority. This is characterized as increasing the "credibility of the government's promises" including the enforcement of property rights (Voight, Ebeling, and Blume 2007). Policies are affected as court decisions build up over time in an "accretive fashion" (Taylor 2005, 5) making analysis of the decisions of the court particularly important. Credibility is important to a state in three broad categories of conflict: (1) cases between state and citizens, (2) cases between private citizens, and (3) cases between branches of government. Voight, Ebeling, and Blume (2007) assert that an independent judiciary could be interpreted as a state commitment to making its promises credible that would extend to both restrained state power (e.g., expropriation) and respect for property rights. On the other hand, if this is not the focus of the state then appeals will be abolished. A leadership more interested in using resources for its own interests or rent seeking results in what is characterized by Mamdani (1996) as "decentralized despotism" where the state prefers to be free of a final court over which it has no control such as the Privy Council. The quality and credibility of the court itself seems not to be an issue as there has been no perceivable deterioration in those areas of the court itself. It is worth remembering that the twelve members of the Privy Council also serve as the justices on the U.K.'s highest court—The Supreme Court of Judicature.

STRUCTURE OF THE CCJ

The CCJ is an integral part of the agreement that established CARICOM. The goal of the relevant section of agreement is further regional integration on the level of the common law and judicial structure.

In 2003, Caribbean leaders met in Jamaica to ratify the Agreement Establishing the CCJ. Based on this agreement, the CCJ has both original and appellate jurisdictions. Eight nations (Barbados, Belize, Dominica, Guyana, Jamaica, St. Lucia, St. Vincent and the Grenadines, and Trinidad and Tobago) of the fourteen nations officially approved the creation of the CCJ. To date, however, only Barbados, Belize, Dominica, and Guyana have severed ties with the Privy Council and acceded to the CCJ. As Dominica replaced the JCPC with the CCJ in 2016, there are not yet a viable number of appeal outcomes to compare the two courts. As such, the period of descriptive analysis ends at January 1, 2016.

The CCJ is directly governed by the Agreement Establishing the CCJ (Caribbean Community Secretariat 2001). The court has jurisdiction to hear cases between states (original jurisdiction) and appeals of decisions of domestic courts within each state (appellate jurisdiction). If requested by the contracting states, the court has the authority under its original jurisdiction to issue advisory opinions interpreting and applying the Treaty of Chaguaramas that establishes CARICOM. The president of the court is joined by not more than nine judges established by Article V of agreement. Each member serves for a nonrenewable term of seven years or until the age seventy-two. Judges sit in panels of three or five under the authority and direction of the president or senior judge on panel. Although there is no quota of justices from any CARICOM state, justices do not represent their state of origin nor is there a requirement that the justice hail from any particular CARICOM member; the court is remarkably diverse. Candidates are considered from any CARICOM member state not just those who accede to the CCJ. Justices hail from St. Kitts and Nevis (Sir Charles Michael Dennis Byron, President of the CCJ), St. Vincent and the Grenadines (The Honourable Mr. Justice Adrian Dudley Saunders), Curacao (The Honourable Mr. Justice Wit), U.K. (The Honourable Mr. Justice David Hayton), Jamaica (The Honourable Mr. Justice Winston Charles Anderson), Trinidad and Tobago (The Honorable Mme. Justice Rajnauth-Lee), and Belize (The Honourable Mr. Justice Denys Barrow). From its inception in 2005 to 2018, four justices have retired, and new justices confirmed by the Regional Judicial and Legal Services Commission (RJLSCO). The RJLSCO was established in accordance with the Article V (1) of the Agreement Establishing the CCJ ratified in 2001. Other important structural aspects of the court include Code of Judicial Conduct, CCJ Trust Fund, administrative staff, a Court Registry, official court calendar, Court Library, and the Caribbean Academy for Law & Court Administration (The Caribbean Court of Justice. n.d). An important aspect of the court is the ability to adjudicate live via the internet. Further, e-filling is available via a folio portal.[3] These facilities give the court the ability to handle fillings, interlocutory matters, and deliver decisions of the court without the parties having to travel to the physical court located in Port of Spain, Trinidad and Tobago. The internet proceedings can be viewed by the public in the jurisdictions involved in the case in a courtroom setting. The importance of this facility cannot be overestimated when one considers the distances between the states. For example, the distance from Belize to Trinidad and Tobago is 1,883 miles (3,030 kilometers).

CHALLENGES FOR THE CCJ

Two critical areas attract attention particularly when compared to the JCPC. First is the selection and seating of judges. As the Law Lords on the JCPC are members of the highest court of the U.K., the Supreme Court of Judicature, their appointments are completely at the discretion of the British government. States that allow appeals to the JCPC have no input. This is viewed as important to independence and impartiality and an argument in some states for retaining the court. For example, in an interview, the former President of The Bahamian Bar Association, Ruth Bowe Darville, explicitly supports the retention of the JCPC (Rolle 2012). Darville points out that those who advocate the removal of the JCPC are "treading in very dangerous waters," as "litigants who come before us with multimillion dollar cases and they see us as a great financial center, they need assurance that the Privy Council [JCPC] is there" (as cited by Rolle 2012, para. 4). In other words, the JCPC is needed to demonstrate and reinforce the independence of the judiciary to those with economic interest in The Bahamas. This argument is reminiscent of that used by the sectors of the business community in New Zealand. John Hagan, Chairman of Deloitte Touché Tohmatsu, spoke on behalf of his and four other accounting firms. He asserted that commercial interests would be subject to a biased and less competent domestic court. Finally, Robert Kerr, Chairman of the New Zealand Business Round Table, reiterated confidence in the JCPC, particularly regarding commercial cases, and expressed skepticism about the attorney general's process of consultation about its domestic replacement (Kerr 2002).

The composition of the body responsible for seating judges reflects a significant effort to minimize bias or individual state interesting in the process. Article V (Caribbean Community Secretariat 2001) provides for the establishment of the RJLSCO[4] with responsibility for seating judges as vacancies. Ex officio membership is diverse and specifically provides:

There is hereby established a RLSCO which shall consist of the following persons:

(a) The president who shall be the chairman of the commission,
(b) Two persons nominated jointly by the Organisation of the Commonwealth Caribbean Bar Association (OCCBA) and the Organisation of Eastern Caribbean States (OECS) Bar Association,
(c) One chairman of the Judicial Services Commission of a Contracting Party selected in rotation in the English alphabetical order for a period of three years,
(d) The chairman of a Public Service Commission of a Contracting Party selected in rotation in the reverse English alphabetical order for a period of three years,
(e) Two persons from civil society nominated jointly by the Secretary-General of the Community and the Director General of the OECS for a period of three years following consultations with regional nongovernmental organizations,
(f) Two distinguished jurists nominated jointly by the Dean of the Faculty of Law of the University of the West Indies, the Deans of the Faculties of Law of any of the Contracting Parties, and the Chairman of the Council of Legal Education,
and
(g) Two persons nominated jointly by the Bar or Law Associations of the Contracting Parties (4).

The second is funding for the court. States that allow appeals to the JCPC have no direct fiscal responsibility for the court which is funded by the British government. The appellant's (and respondent if appearing before court) costs lie in accessing the court in London (e.g., travel, accommodations, legal counsel etc.). Article XXVII provides for how the court is funded by the states. States must write payment into law and all funds into a consolidated fund which is administered by a Board of Trustees. Currently, the fund sits at U.S. $100 million (Caribbean Court of Justice 2012). There are also important protections for the salaries and allowance for the judges during tenure. The Board of Trustees is also an array of ex officio members representing CARICOM's legal, educational, and business elite (Caribbean Court of Justice 2012):

- The Secretary-General (of the CARICOM),
- The Vice-Chancellor of the University of the West Indies,
- The President of the Insurance Association of the Caribbean,
- The Chairman of the Association of Indigenous Banks of the Caribbean,
- The President of the Caribbean Institute of Chartered Accountants,
- The President of the Organisation of Commonwealth Caribbean Bar Associations,

- The Chairman of the Conference of Heads of the Judiciary of Member States of the CARICOM,
- The President of the Caribbean Association of Industry and Commerce, and
- The President of the Caribbean Congress of Labour.

These provisions represent a thoughtful effort to dilute the influence of any single state and detach the membership from direct political influences to bolster the independence of the court. The fact that only four of the twelve states have acceded to the CCJ (appellate jurisdiction) since inception in 2005 signals the challenges the court faces in establishing itself as a viable alternative to the JCPC.

The challenge for the CCJ is not just structural. The states face many issues when attempting to accede to the CCJ. This issue of the death penalty is salient as all Anglophone member of CARICOM retained the death penalty and are among the 58 countries that retain the death sentence at law while 140 countries have abolished it by law or de facto by refraining to carry out the sentence (Amnesty International 2016). The JCPC has played a critical role in changing the course of Caribbean jurisprudence in the last twenty-five years starting with *Pratt and Morgan v the Attorney General of Jamaica* (1993).[5] On January 15, 1979, the Supreme Court of Jamaica convicted Earl Pratt and Ivan Morgan of murder and sentenced them to death. They remained in prison for fourteen years during the appeal process. On three occasions, the authorities read their death warrants and transferred them to the condemned cells immediately adjacent to the gallows. In 1993, Jamaica's final appellate court, the JCPC, heard their appeal. The court concluded that this delay constituted cruel and unusual punishment and commuted the death sentence to life imprisonment. This case is significant in Caribbean jurisprudence as it is the first time the court has explicitly adopted a standard for cruel and unusual punishment based on delays in carrying out the death penalty. The court goes further by setting a threshold of five years on death row after which execution could be cruel and unusual punishment. The JCPC's preferences are made abundantly clear in the Belizean case, *Reyes v. The Queen* (2002).[6] Lord Bingham of Cornwall in delivering the decision states,

> A generous and purposive interpretation is to be given to constitutional provisions protecting human rights. The court has no license to read its own predilections and moral values into the Constitution, but it is required to consider the substance of the fundamental right at issue and ensure contemporary protection of that right in the light of evolving standards of decency that mark the progress of a maturing society. (26)

This implies that while the justices must follow the Constitution of the country, they are "required" to interpret it in the context of the times. As their rulings are not subject to review by any other court, it raises the specter of policy-making by this court (Stone Sweet 2000).

This induced a public backlash in the Caribbean with the general sentiment being one of support for the death penalty and unhappiness with JCPC decisions on that issue (Anthony 2003). A dispute over capital punishment or judicial imperialism by the region's highest appellate court can also be understood as a response to the over-legalization of the governments' human rights commitments (Heifer 2002). Caribbean governments, for their part, see the death penalty as a "vote-winner" with the electorate. With that in mind plans have gone ahead to replace the Privy Council with the CCJ (Mills 2005). The popular majorities support the mandatory death penalty in the belief that it acts as a deterrent to violent crime. The possibility of its abolition by a panel composed of judges thousands of miles away is a highly sensitive issue politically. Some observers argue that it should be for the countries' parliaments, and not distant judges, to decide whether the mandatory death sentence should be abolished. Death penalty opponents fear that the CCJ will not amount to anything more than a "hangman's court" allowing for regional states to carry out the death penalty (Richards 2006).

The public discourse in the Bahamas is exemplary of the bifurcated discussion about acceding to the CCJ. Following the JCPC's decision in *Maxo Tido v The Queen* (2011)[7] to overturn the death penalty sentence handed down by the domestic court of appeals in 2002, a former President of The Bahamian Bar Association, Ruth Bowe Darville, was reported as saying, "I think the question of the death penalty needs to be addressed. I think the country is torn by it because we're in the throes of this crime epidemic as people have labeled it" (as cited by McCartney June 25, 2011, para. 12). Darville suggested that the issue of the death penalty be addressed through legislation but with the knowledge that care must be taken not to offend the international community and that any action is linked to the economic well-being of The Bahamas. Religious leaders presented another view of the issue. While Toote (2013) asserts that most of the Bahamians supported the death penalty, an important divide existed in the religious leadership. The Anglican Bishop and the Methodist synod came out against the death penalty (Toote 2013). In 2009, the Roman Catholic Archbishop reaffirmed the Church's stance against the death penalty (BahamaCatholic 2009). However, most Baptists, the single largest denomination in The Bahamas at 40 percent of the population, supported the death penalty (Toote 2013).

Only a minority of politicians came out publicly in support of the death penalty (Toote 2013). Not surprisingly, therefore, the reaction of the governing coalition is cautious. It tries to separately address the issues of the death penalty and any calls to completely abolish appeals to the JCPC. In addition, unlike the very public position in favor of abolishing appeals to the JCPC taken by the Labour Party's Manifesto for New Zealand, the approach of the political party leading the governing coalition and the opposition party reflects the bifurcated approach to the issue of the JCPC. In its Charter of Governance, the governing PLP acknowledged that death penalty decisions of the JCPC constrained the state's ability to enforce the death penalty. Instead of calling for the abolition of the JCPC, it pledged to ensure "that all avenues of appeal are exhausted without delay. Cases that are complete and warrant the death penalty shall be deposed of expeditiously . . . fast-tracked to the Supreme Court to ensure that our laws are no longer reduced to bluffs" (Progressive Liberal Party 2011). This was a commitment by the governing coalition to follow the rule of law. It was also a pledge to abide by the JCPC precedent set in *Pratt and Another v. Attorney General and Another* (1993) that overturned the death penalty sentence on the grounds of undue delay. The opposition FNM makes two main promises in the party's manifesto. First, it promises to reduce delays in the prosecution of criminal cases (Manifesto '07, 4). Second, in a 2014 speech, the Honorary Dr. Hubert A Minnis (then Leader of the Opposition) promises to introduce a bill that would mandate that "an appeal against a sentence of death can only be made to the Bahamas Court of Appeal, and nowhere else" (Minnis 2014, para. 35). Such a constitutional amendment would effectively oust the jurisdiction of the JCPC specifically but only in death penalty cases. This approach was an effort to recognize voter support for the death penalty, and to retain the JCPC for all other matters to reassure those interested in retaining the JCPC as a hallmark of credibility and independence of the Bahamian judiciary. To date no such bill has been introduced to the Bahamian Parliament.

Other jurisdictions have had other issues. In St. Vincent and the Grenadines, a 2015 referendum on constitutional changes which include replacing the JCPC with the JCC failed to garner a majority vote. A 2016 referendum in Grenada also failed to win majority support. In the two most populous jurisdictions, Jamaica and Trinidad and Tobago, the issue has been a political football. Political parties have championed the change only to renege later siting various reasons. Then prime minister of Trinidad and Tobago, Mrs. Persad-Bissessar, explained that the JCPC inspired international confidence in her country that encourage foreign investors. This vacillation led the former prime minister of Jamaica, Mr. P.J. Patterson, to remark, "There can be no valid reason why the CCJ cannot be asked by its two most populous member states, who have contributed substantially to its funding, why the CCJ cannot be asked to take responsibility for its final jurisdiction in full" (Fraser n.d.).

Over the thirteen years, however, the CCJ continues to see increasing number of appeals and growing docket. This extraterrestrial regional court is assuming a growing jurisdiction as states accede expanding the role as the final judicial adjudicator of intra and interstate conflicts. A window to how the court approaching this important role in Caribbean jurisprudence is encapsulated in the dissenting opinion of Justice Witt in *August and Gabb v. The Queen* (2018)[8]:

> The standard of review must therefore be as broad and liberal as possible and the appellate courts in Belize, both the Court of Appeal and this Court as the final court of appeal, have a duty to be proactive in their handling of appeals against conviction, just as the Legislature intended. We simply cannot afford to follow the conservative and narrow approach of the English courts, lest we create or maintain injustice. (75)

To date, the CCJ has adjudicated 157 matters. Number of appeals adjudicated by four states since acceding to CCJ and the JCPC for the other nine states between 2005 and 2017 are presented in Table 4.1. Some of the decisions have impacted Caribbean jurisprudence and further entrenched regional integration efforts. In thirteen years with the CCJ, Barbados and Guyana have each had sixty-nine appeals adjudicated. That is an average of 5.3 appeals per year. Before the JCPC, forty-four Jamaican and seventy-four Appeals from Trinidad and Tobago have been adjudicated over fifty-six years. This is 0.8 average per year for Jamaica and 1.3 average per year for Trinidad and Tobago. Two reasons are suggested higher yearly average at the CCJ by Barbados and Guyana verses Jamaica and Trinidad and Tobago (more people and larger economies) at the JCPC. First, the CCJ is more accessible with the court in Trinidad and Tobago and live closed circuit proceedings in each jurisdiction. Second, the comparative willingness of the CCJ to accept appeals to establish reputable

Table 4.1 Number of Appeals Adjudicated by Four States since Acceding to CCJ and the JCPC for the Other Nine States between 2005 and 2017

States (4)	*Year Acceded to CCJ*	*No. of Appeals Adjudicated*
Barbados	2005 (13 years)	69
Belize	2010 (8 years)	20
Dominica	2016 (1 year)	0
Guyana	2005 (13 years)	69
States (9)	Years with JCPC	
Antigua and Barbuda	37 years	9
Bahamas	45 years	27
Dominica	38 years	4
Grenada	44 years	4
Jamaica	56 years	44
St. Kitts and Nevis	37 years	8
St. Lucia	39 years	5
St. Vincent	39 years	5
Trinidad and Tobago	56 years	74

and consolidate its position in the Caribbean. If and how the court changes to be more selective in controlling its docket is a subject for future examination.

A salient issue is the death penalty with opponents of the death penalty fearing the CCJ would be a hangman court. These fears have not materialized, and the death penalty remains in the laws of all Anglophone Caribbean states. This issue is addressed by the prime minister of St. Lucia, Dr. the Honourable Kenny D. Anthony (2003) who, in supporting the establishment of the court, states,

> By far the most troubling criticism of the Court, has been the suggestion that the CCJ is a cynical attempt on the part of some Caribbean politicians to facilitate hanging of death row inmates across the region. . . . The issues are separate and moreover, while the argument is convenient, it has distracted from discussion of what I consider are more salient concerns, namely insulating the Court from political interference and guaranteeing its financial integrity and independence. (Anthony 2003, paras. 21, 28)

COMPARING OUTCOMES: WINNER AND LOSERS

If courts must be understood as part of the political and judicial decision-making process, their decision will produce winners and losers. In other words, those who the court's decision favors get what they want with the other party does not. While the research varies on the significance and role the judicial system plays in making public policy, they all agree that the courts do have a role. The expanding role of the political institutions in the activities of the state leads to a correspondingly larger role for the courts. Whether a declaration of right as part of mobilization by legal activists (Scheingold 1974) or in tension with administrators or the public where the law functions as a discretion-reinforcing agent (Cooper 1985), the judiciary plays a role in policy-making.

It can, therefore, also be assumed that when the state is a party in a case, the states wants the court to support their policies. Dahl (1957) asserts that national governing coalitions desire a high court (the U.S. Supreme Court) to act as an ally and uphold its policies. The court decisions may not have the same role in every issue, but judicially asserted rights are authoritatively articulated goals of public policy and more useful when used as an agent of political mobilization (Scheingold 1974).

When the countries gained independence, many constitutions included provisions that saved the laws enacted by colonial legislatures as existing laws (Ghany 2000) in Caribbean Commonwealth countries. The saved laws included the death penalty for capital crimes. Along with Guatemala, Cuba, and the United States, the Commonwealth Caribbean states are the only

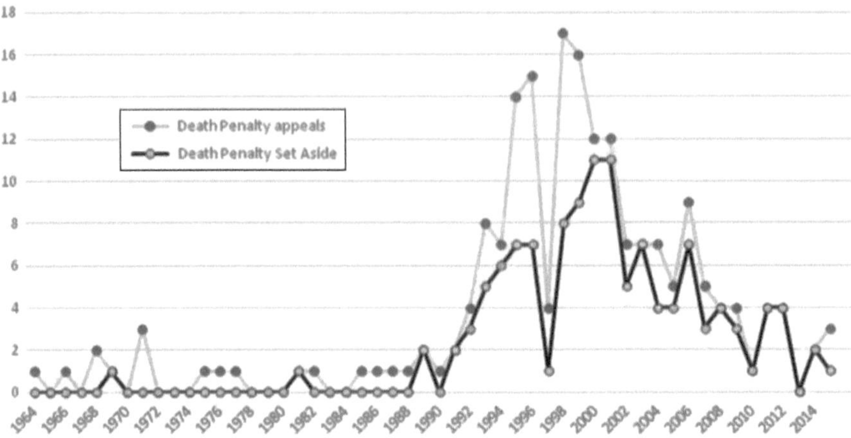

Figure 4.1 The Number of Appeals and the Comparative Numbers When the Death Penalty Was Set Aside by the JCPC from 1964 to 2014.

nations in the Americas to retain the death penalty as a form of legal sanction. Further, the Commonwealth Caribbean countries are among the 58 countries that retain the death sentence at law while 140 countries have abolished it by law or de facto by refraining to carry out the sentence (Amnesty International 2016). The courts in the Caribbean continued to sentence people to death and appeals continue to the JCPC. Figure 4.1 presents the number of appeals and the comparative numbers when the death penalty was set aside by the court from 1964 to 2014. This review of appeals shows an uptick in death penalty appeals to the JCPC from 1992 to 2002. The uptick accompanies an increase in the number of appeals in which the death penalty was set aside. Even with the declining number of appeals starting in 2002, the comparative numbers of appeals in which the death penalty is set aside remains high (BBC World News 2007; Harrington 2004). The decline in appeals is partially attributable to the fact that three states—Barbados, Belize, and Guyana—have replaced the JCPC with the CCJ.

For those states that have acceded to the CCJ, fears of the death penalty opponents have not come to fruition. In *The Attorney General, Superintendent of Prisons and Chief Marshal v. Jeffrey Joseph and Lennox Ricardo Boyce* (2006),[9] a death penalty case from Barbados, the court followed the JCPC precedents established in *Pratt and Morgan v Attorney General of Jamaica and Other* (1993) and *Boyce v. the Queen* (2004).[10] The court upheld the appeal that the mandatory death sentence as unconstitutional. The court noted that Barbados passed a constitutional amendment to further entrench the death penalty but had failed resolve the contradictions in the case law involving the approximate five-year time lapse in carrying out the death penalty after which it is no longer mandatory (*Pratt and Morgan* 1993) and the need for a clemency hearing (*Lewis v. The Attorney General of Barbados* 2000[11]). Further, in *August and Gabb v. The Queen* (2018), the majority held that the mandatory minimum life sentence as prescribed in section 106 (1) of the Criminal Code of Belize is unconstitutional. To date, the decisions have not visibly mobilized the anti-death penalty supporters nor dampened the calls by those who wish for it to be used more often.

With the JCPC sitting in London and staffed and funded by the British government, there has always had the air of independence of any state from which a case originates. The notion that this is beneficial to the domestic judicial system and the state generally is echoed in several corners of the British Commonwealth. The former President of The Bahamian Bar Association comments (cited in Rolle 2012) discussed above suggest that the option of appealing to JCPC reinforces the independence of the Bahamian judiciary in the eyes of foreign investors. This sentiment is echoed in New Zealand as it contemplated abandoning the JCPC (Kerr 2002). Three years after independence in 1964, then prime minister Lee Kuan Yew of Singapore stated that the retention of the JCPC was a sign to the world of a commitment to judicial independence (Seow 1997; Tan 2015). The statement of then prime minister Lee Kuan Yew to parliament in 1967 is clear:

> As long as governments are wise enough to leave alone the rights of appeal to some superior body outside Singapore, then there must be a higher degree of confidence in the integrity of our judicial process. This is most important. (Cited in Seow 1997, para. 15)

There is no denying the judicial experience, quality and the prestige attributed to the JCPC and that for some of the new states continued affiliation with the JCPC conferred some degree of legitimacy to their judicial system. The quality of the JCPC decisions is an important part of its credibility and the high quality of the Law Lords and their decisions is not seriously questioned in the literature. The CCJ is still working to establish its reputation for impartial adjudication. Compared to the centuries behind the JCPC, the thirteen-year existence of the CCJ is short but not insignificant. A comparative approach is used with appeals in which the state is a party to detect any overt bias in the outcomes. Included are the nine Caribbean states with 185 appeals to the JCPC and the three Caribbean states with 49 appeals to the CCJ between 2005 (the year the CCJ started hearing appeals) and 2017. Figure 4.2 presents the number of appeals, the percentage favoring the state and where the court varied the judgment of the lower court. In this context, a decision is categorized as varied when only a part of the appeal is upheld. A poignant example is when the conviction and death penalty are on appeal and the court

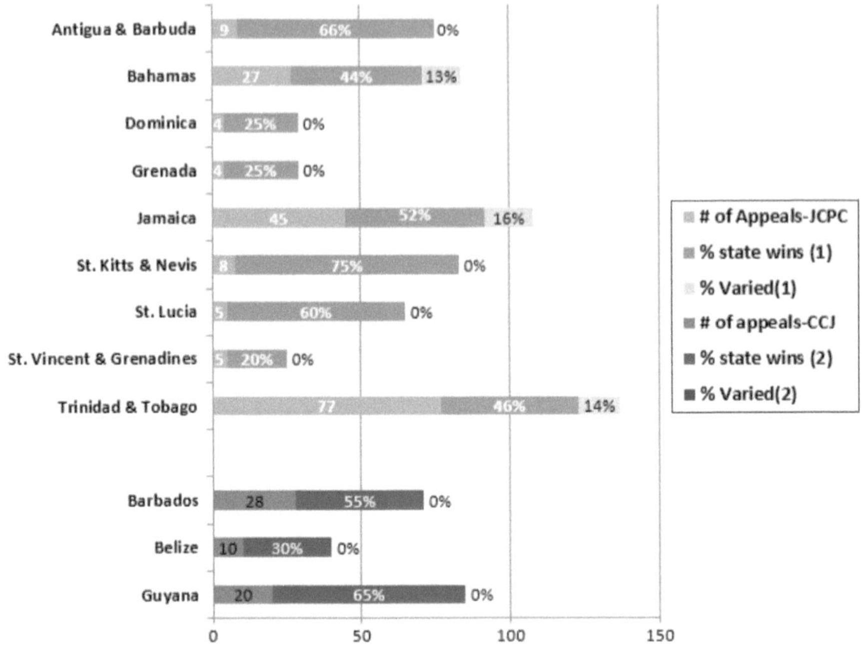

Figure 4.2 Percentage of Appeals Won by the State (Appellant or Appellee) before the JCPC (Nine States from 2005 to 2017) and CCJ (Three States from 2005 to 2017).

upholds the conviction but commutes the death sentence or remits the case to the lower court for sentencing. The first nine countries retain appeals to the JCPC and the last three (Barbados, Belize, and Guyana) appeal to the CCJ.

The analysis reveals that the nine states are successful, on average, at the JCPC 46 percent (46 Median, S.D. 19.5) of the time while the three states with appeals to the CCJ are, on average, successful 50 percent (Median 55, S.D. 18) of the time. This shows a remarkable consistency between the two courts with no central tendency in favor of the states. Also, of note is that the states are the Respondent in 98 percent of the appeals before the JCPC and 88 percent before the CCJ. This willingness to challenge the state in the highest legal forum is a good sign of the growing trust in the court. It also retains the relevance of the judiciary as an avenue to check the legislative and executive branches of government.

CONCLUSION

As the regional court for the last thirteen years to only four of the fourteen CARICOM states have acceded. While hesitation by Surinam and Haiti as the only two civil law jurisdictions in a sea of common-law jurisdictions, there is no legal barrier to the other states severing ties with the JCPC and acceding to the CCJ more than the confidence and political will to do pass the constitutional amendment. It is particularly interesting that two largest jurisdiction, Jamaica and Trinidad and Tobago, have not acceded. Further, the court itself is in Port of Spain, Trinidad. President Carmona of Trinidad and Tobago (Caribbean360 August 25, 2017) links the sealing of a Caribbean identity with states acceding to the court declaring,

> Perhaps the day will finally come when we can all take pride in, and responsibility for, defining, shaping, writing and ultimately, rewriting our own jurisprudence and laws in the context of our own peculiarities and the relationships among our own member states. The arguments for a common jurisprudence have been exhausted but are not exhaustible. (para. 6)

Two years after the proposal to accede was defeated in the 2016 national referendum in Grenada, Prime Minister Dr. Keith Mitchell (CMC. March 26, 2018) states that,

> as it relates to our independence and to our national identity, we must open up a dialogue again, about our joining the Caribbean Court of Justice . . . this land that gave birth to revolutionaries Julien Fedon and Henri Christophe; this land that gave birth to leaders who were fathers of Grenada's independence and defenders of its place in the world, such as Eric Gairy and Maurice Bishop; this land must and shall do better than we have done on this issue. . . . Today, I call for a re-opening of the dialogue on the CCJ and the development of a united front in going forward—for this issue should not divide us along lines of neither party nor class. (paras. 2, 8, and 9)

Although Barbados was the second state to accede to the CCJ, leading up to general election in April 2018, Prime Minster Stuart states, "Once the Democratic Labour Party (DLP) is returned to office, Barbados will be withdrawing from the Caribbean Court of Justice (CCJ) as its final Court of Appeal" (Alphonse, May 20, 2018). The DLP lost all thirty seats in parliament on May 28, 2018, and Mia Motley became the first female Prime Minster of Barbados with a continued commitment to the CCJ.

These recent developments indicate that the domestic discourse is alive and well in many of the states. Further, opinion leaders are following and addressing development is other states. The comparative examination of the court outcomes shows the CCJ has been remarkably consistent with the outcome of the JCPC between 2005 and 2017 where the states are a party to the appeal. This may serve to assuage those who may question the independence of the CCJ and the integrity of the justices. This does not mean that the governments will always be pleased with rulings of the court. This is clear in the remarks of the then Prime Minister of Barbados, Freundel Stuart, leading up to parliamentary elections in May 2018 (Alphonse May 20, 2018). He states,

> I am not going to have Barbados disrespected by politicians wearing robes. I don't subscribe to disrespect and I think that the attitude coming from Port of Spain leaves much to be desired in terms of how it is treating Barbados. (para. 3)

It would be unusual for there not to be any tensions between states and the extraterritorial court. As other CARICOM states deliberate or vacillate on joining the CCJ, this is expected to continue. The singularity of the CCJ, however, extends beyond having appellate and original jurisdiction under treaty discussed earlier in this chapter. First, the method of selection justices via ex officio members from a wide variety of regional and domestic organizations goes a long way to insulate the court from the weighted influence of any state. Second, the tenure of justices' balances consistency and stability with vacancies and replacements. Finally, funding of the court is held away from political whims with states contributions going to the consolidated fund administered by ex officio trustees. It remains to be seen, however, the level of importance and commitment each state invests in changing the status quo. The Bahamas has explicit signaled that it will not consider joining the CCJ. While there are intermittent rumbling in Jamaica and Trinidad and Tobago about acceding to the court, neither has done so as yet. Nevertheless, outside of EU, the CCJ remains not just a relevant part of CARICOM and viable alternative to the JCPC but a model for other regional integration efforts.

NOTES

1. On December 15, 1965, at Dickenson Bay in Antigua, prime ministers Forbes Burnham of Guyana, Errol Barrow of Barbados, and Vere Bird of Antigua signed the Dickenson Bay Agreement laying the foundation for the Caribbean Free Trade Area (CARIFTA). The High Road to the Caribbean Community. 2017. *The Integrationist Caribbean*. Accessed June 17, 2019.
http://www.theintegrationistcaribbean.org/feature/the-high-road-to-the-caribbean-community/.
2. Chaguaramas is a coastal area and inlet on the North West Peninsula of Trinidad about fifteen miles west of Port of Spain which is the capital of Trinidad and Tobago.
3. The Folio portal was enacted by Practice Direction 1 of 2016. The Caribbean Court of Justice. *E-Filling*. Accessed June 18, 2019. http://www.ccj.org/e-filing-portal/.
4. The RJLSC is an independent, nonpolitical body of eleven persons. It is responsible for the selection, hiring and discipline, and fixing the terms and conditions of employment of the Court's staff (Caribbean Court of Justice. n.d.).

5. *Pratt and Morgan v Attorney General of Jamaica and Other*. 1993. 43 WIR 340.
6. *Reyes v. The Queen*. 2002. 60 WIR 26.
7. *Maxo Tido v The Queen*. 16 UKPC 2011.
8. *August and Gabb v. The Queen* [2018] CCJ 7 (AJ).
9. *The Attorney General, Superintendent of Prisons and Chief Marshal and Jeffrey Joseph and Lennox Ricardo Boyce*. 2006 CCJ 3 (AJ).
10. *Boyce v. the Queen*. [2004] UKPC 32.
11. *Lewis v Attorney-General of Barbados*. 2000. 57 WIR 275.

Chapter 5

Summary and the Future Extraterritorial Courts

SUMMARY

In an era of increasing globalization and regional integration, the emergence and continuing relevance of extraterritorial courts does not seem to be in doubt. This is a form of outsourcing dispute resolution to forums in the form of shared appellate courts. Such courts challenge the traditional idea of state sovereignty. Traditionally, states retain domestic control over judicial institutions. It reflects the part of the globalization which pierces the domestic judicial system and creates links to an extraterritorial sphere of adjudication.

While the literature on ECJ is increasing, there is a gap in our understanding of the development of extraterritorial courts outside of Europe and the broader regional integration through the European Community (Garrett, Keleman, and Schulz 1998). This book contributes to our understanding of how governing coalitions view courts in terms of the broader construction and understanding of the state in the era of globalization and the emergence of new extraterritorial courts. Countries that have a domestic final appellate court have established a judicial institution over which they have control as part of the policy-making governing structure. How they view other existing and emerging extraterritorial courts will be influenced by their perception of the court and the role it will play when the policies of the governing coalition are challenged. When legal challenges arise, the governing coalition ultimately wants its policies to be upheld and legitimized by the court. Justice Jallow notes that the "judiciary, therefore, functions to ensure legality, fairness, accountability and objectivity in the process of governing" (as cited by Senghore 2010, 216).

The ongoing interest in regional and global efforts to foster international law and legal tribunals is an important part of globalization. As Slaughter

(2000) points out, “Globalization summons images more of corporations than courts . . . notwithstanding this perception, judges are globalizing as well, in ways that have important implications for foreign, comparative and international law” (1103). This phenomenon is observed in diverse regions of the world. An institution of the Organization of American States (OAS), the ICAHR received seventy-seven petitions from twelve states in 2016. In 2017, the court received 111 applications from 20 states, a 31 percent increase in petitions (Inter-American Commission on Human Rights 2016). The African Court on Human and Peoples’ Rights (established by the AU in 2006) received seven petitions in 2013 (African Court of Human and People’s Rights 2013). In 2016, however, the commission received fifty-seven petitions representing an 89 percent increase (African Court of Human and People’s Rights 2017). This book focuses on two extraterritorial courts—the JCPC and the CCJ. The JCPC is linked to the British Commonwealth state by history and choice and the CCJ emerged as part of Caribbean’s regional integration agreement, CARICOM.

Chapter 1 presents the history of the JCPC and the role it plays in the British Empire and in the British Commonwealth. Extraterritorial courts such as the ECJ, ECtHR, and African Court on Human and People’s Rights (ACHPR) do not have the 400-year tradition and reputation that contributed to the propensity of former British colonies to retain the JCPC at independence. The JCPC has a long history of involvement in the jurisprudence of colonies and former colonies around the world and is arguably the first extraterritorial court. The judicial experience, quality, and the prestige attributed to the JCPC are beyond question. In fact, the quality of the JCPC decisions is an important part of its credibility and the high quality of the Law Lords. While their decisions may spawn disagreements about the interpretation of law, the court’s credibility is not seriously questioned in the literature. Of the fifty former colonies examined, twenty states abolished appeals to the JCPC at independence, eighteen states retained but then replaced it at different times, and twelve states retained right of appeal as of January 1, 2018. For many new states, continued affiliation with the JCPC confers some degree of legitimacy onto their own judicial system. This influences retention at independence; subsequent efforts of Commonwealth Caribbean states to transition away from that court to the CCJ is a unique case study.

Chapter 2 first examines the relationship between fifty colonies at independence and the JCPC. This is the first critical junction where the governing coalition has the option of retaining appeals to the JCPC, continuing the role of the colonial institution as the final appellate. Thirty of the fifty colonies retained JCPC at independence. This supports the assertion of institutional path dependency and the significance of the length of colonial rule that entrenches the institutions reducing the likelihood of abandoning appeals to the JCPC at independence. This link to the colonial ruler persists in many states for varying lengths of time despite other aspects of sovereignty assumed at independence.

The results of the analysis of the JCPC and British Commonwealth states, at the first critical junction at independence, have two major implications. First, the strength of the ties between the state and the extraterritorial court is influenced by how long the relationship has existed. The longer the relationship between the state and the extraterritorial court, the more difficult it is for the governing coalition to marshal the political will to sever ties. In other words, the longer the extraterritorial courts are utilized by the state, the less likely the state is to sever ties later. The average length of colony status for the states included in this research is 121 years, and this duration and relative strength of the colonial influence greatly contributed to the decision on the status of the JCPC during the decolonization process. For example, only two of the twenty states (10%) that experienced colonial rule longer than the average, abolished the JCPC. Of the thirty states that retained the JCPC at independence, thirteen states (43%) experienced shorter than the average length of colonial rule. New courts, therefore, must have time on their said for institutional stickiness to set in and dissuade defection by the states. Second, the perception of the reliability of the extraterritorial court is influenced by the decisions of the courts and the domestic political environment. The findings suggest that individual JCPC decisions unfavorable to the state and changes in the political environment are not the only factors influencing the governing coalitions to establish final appellate courts they expect to be a reliable partner in furthering its policies. Rather, it is the convergence of these factors which may lead the governing coalition in each state to abolish appeals to the JCPC and establish a domestic final appellate court. Any court is well advised to exercise judicial restraint. In other words, the courts need to answer the legal questions before them and refrain to extending judgments into areas more appropriately handled in the political sphere. Ultimately, therefore, the state's commitment to the continued jurisdiction of the court is predicated on the expectation that in a specific political environment its policies are likely to be upheld. If this is not realized, the courts are more likely to be considered expendable.

Findings suggest that the persistence of the institution after independence depends on how deeply embedded the JCPC is in the governing structures of the state. While the governing coalition does necessarily pay attention to specific decisions of the court, its ability to tolerate unfavorable decisions—or even the possibility of unfavorable decisions—is influenced by the domestic political environment. It can be argued, however, that in the case of India, retaining the JCPC at independence only to sever ties within two years was designed to signal continuity and a sense of stability during a tumultuous period of Indian independence, the creation of Pakistan and giving the court time to deliver decisions on pending appeals. Conversely, New Zealand retained the JCPC for sixty-four years after it had the option to server in 1931. St. Kitts was a colony for over three centuries and still retains the JCPC three decades after independence. Both these latter countries transition away from colonial rule without conflict and remain stable democracies.

The critical juncture at independence, therefore, is an opportunity for new state's governing coalitions to achieve their goal of establishing a new institutional equilibrium. These decisions by newly independent nations to retain or replace the JCPC are a part of that larger effort. The broader implication is that while states remain publicly interested in the jurisdiction of extraterritorial courts and the relationship with the state, their commitment to actually accepting the jurisdiction of these courts is influenced by the states' perception of where their own interests lie and whether the courts will ultimately support their policies. States seem unwilling to merely push for renegotiation of the administrative and institutional structures; instead they will sever ties with the extraterritorial court. This is exemplified by South Africa which withdrew from the International Criminal Court, asserting United Nation's Security Council bias in referring only African cases (Strydom October 15, 2015; Duggard 2013). Individuals can be referred to this extraterritorial court and tried when the state refuses or is unable to prosecute to do so itself. African criticisms of the ICC charge that the ICC has "lost its direction" (Strydom 2015, para. 1) pointing to the fact that the security council has referred cases involving individuals from Sudan and Libya, while situations such as those in Syria and Israel have not been referred. The suggestion is that there is a distinct bias against Africa (Duggard 2013). Since the establishment of the ICC, only black Africans, particularly high-level officials and politicians (du Plessis, Maluwa, and O'Reilly 2013), have been charged (BBC 2015). The U.K. has threatened to withdraw from the ECJ after decisions in extradition cases were considered unfavorable by the governing Conservative Party (Watt 2015).

In Africa, the East African Court of Appeal (EACA) was agreed to in 1966. It served Kenya, Uganda, and Tanzania. EACA (1967–1977) emerged from a colonial court of appeal, only to be abandoned later by the member states (Harvard Law School Library 2014; Katende and Kanyeihamba 1973). Katende and Kanyeihamba (1973) attribute this to the fact that "the reactions of the governments to decisions of the Court have not always been favorable" (52). Still, this is not considered the only contributing factor. There were personal disputes among leaders about the integration process—ideological differences among leaders—socialist Tanzania, capitalist Kenya, and Uganda were following a policy of mixed economy; in addition, there were Cold War influences and different levels of economic development (Kawa 2016). These differences obstructed the planning process that could sustain integration and support the court and are instructive in terms of issues to be avoided in the future.

After independence, new states are usually directly responsible for all aspects of governance; so the outsourcing of the final court of appeal to the JCPC is an unusual phenomenon. Chapter 3 examines change in the Commonwealth Caribbean to better provide some insight into what factors influence change in the right of appeal to the JCPC after a possible second critical juncture at which point the state may sever the right of appeal to the JCPC. The focus is on the thirteen Anglophone states, or former British colonies. This has regional importance since these states had the JCPC as the final court of appeal, while they were colonies, but at independence each had the option to retain the JCPC. Beginning in 2005, with the creation of the CCJ, they also had the opportunity to choose a regional extraterritorial court to replace the JCPC.

For the Commonwealth Caribbean, the alternative to the JCPC emerges within the framework of the regional integration movement, CARICOM. The CCJ has been a viable appellate since 2005 as provided for in the Treaty of Chaguaramas (1973). The persistence of the JCPC as a viable appellate court of these states, however, does reveal just how embedded it is in many former colonies state judicial structures, the psyche of the governing coalition and the general population. This is reflected by the fact that only four members of CARICOM have acceded to the court to date. Still, the court has exercised its appellate jurisdiction in 163 appeals and 21 appeals using its original jurisdiction between 2005 and 2017 (Caribbean Court of Justice, 2017). Accepting the jurisdiction of the CCJ is slow, and it remains to be seen whether and when the two most populated former colonies, Jamaica and Trinidad and Tobago, will sever ties with the JCPC in favor of the CCJ.

Chapter 4 provides a comparative overview of the JCPC and structure of the CCJ. The contrast is stark. The states have no say or control over the selection and tenure of Law Lords, administration or funding of the JCPC. The agreement establishing the CCJ reflects CARICOM's effort to establish a court reflecting the region but with institutions that minimize the influence of any single state over the court. The important structural aspects of the court include Regional Judicial and Legal Services Commission, Code of Judicial Conduct, CCJ Trust Fund, administrative staff, a Court Registry, official court calendar, Court Library, and the Caribbean Academy for Law & Court Administration. While the acceding states support the court, its administration is carried out by committees created by the enabling law which provides for ex officio members from across the region. The proximity of the court located in Port of Spain, Trinidad and Tobago, and the use of live-streamed proceeding reduces the cost of accessing the court compared to the JCPC in London.

The analysis of the comparative outcomes in appellate jurisdiction appeals between 2005 and 2015, in which the state is a party, shows no significant difference in the success of the state when appealing to the JCPC or the CCJ. It does indicate that the court decisions have not revealed any significant tendency to favor the states. The instrument creating the court CARICOM's integration effect reflects serious attention to the selecting of justices and funding of the court to avoid perception of individual state bias or undue influence on the court. This does not completely address the concerns of states that have not yet acceded to the CCJ, however. The Bahamas, for example, is particularly concerned in the perceptions of international investors that a court in London is intrinsically preferable. Nevertheless, the discourse in many states considering acceding to the CCJ is ongoing.

THE FUTURE

After thirteen years, the CCJ is worth studying. It is important particularly because it is outside the EU, which is made up of developed contiguous states. These countries face vastly different challenges as geographically scattered, developing countries struggling with domestic governance, the pressures of globalization and the geopolitics of developed states. The court faces many important issues. In July 2018, the murder cases of *Jabari Sensimania Nervais v The Queen* and *Dwayne Omar Severin v The Queen*[1] were consolidated. Both appeals challenged the convictions and the constitutionality of the mandatory death sentence for murder in Barbados. The CCJ finds that the mandatory death sentence is unconstitutional, reversing the JCPC decision in *Boyce v the Queen* (2004).[2] It follows a similar decision in *August and Gabb v. The Queen* (2018)[3] originating in Belize. While no one has been executed in Barbados in thirty-four years or in Belize in thirty years, the number of people on death row has increased.

The salience of lesbian, gay, transgender, bisexual, and queer (LGTBQ) issues are also on the rise. In *McEwan, Clarke, Fraser, Persaud and the Society Against Sexual Orientation Discrimination (SASOD) vs. Attorney General of Guyana* (2018),[4] the CCJ has reserved judgment. This is an appeal from Guyana against the conviction of the four men for wearing women's clothes in violation of the 1893 vagrancy law (Section 153 (1) (XLVII) of the Summary Jurisdiction (Offences) Act Chapter 8:02) outlawing such behavior. While the Supreme Court of Belize found the law against sodomy to be unconstitutional. In *Orozco v. The Attorney General of Belize* (2016),[5] Chief Justice Kenneth Benjamin of Belize held that "laws purporting to criminalize private homosexual conduct breached the rights to dignity, privacy, equality and non-discrimination enshrined in the Belize Constitution and so were void" (Blackstone Chambers August 11, 2016, para. 1; Human Dignity Trust August 10, 2016). This decision is affirmed by the Belize Court of Appeals (Civil Appeal 32 of 2016) in a unanimous decision on December 30, 2019. Similar laws remain the other Commonwealth Caribbean states and an appeal is yet to reach the CCJ for adjudication.

The institution's resilience is being tested in several ways. First, the first cycle of replacing a justice(s) means there will, in effect, be a "new" court very soon. Second, as new states accede it will be important to examine how the court adjusts to the increasing caseload. Docket control will be crucial to maintain the court's focus on the most important legal issues and maintain the quality of opinions. Both these issues are pillars supporting the reputation and prestige of the court. Third, maintaining stable funding and administration also underpins the independence and vitality of the court. Finally, all three are important determinants of whether the states retain the CCJ. As research indicates, states may not respond directly to individual opinions, but trends erode confidence and feed negative perceptions, even of future opinions of the court. Therefore, readers will benefit from future study and evaluation of the CCJ.

Significantly, the ongoing CARCOM integration process is tied to the success of the CCJ and how many countries accede. Still, even at this point, the CCJ is a viable alternative model to the ECJ and ECtHR in the EU for the rest of the world. Only recently, and tentatively, have other regions contemplated establishing regional appellate forums (appellate jurisdiction).

While other regional organizations have some conflict resolution forum in place, they have primarily focused on dispute resolution between the states using primary jurisdictional power. The proposed Statute of the Arab Court of Human Rights was rejected by the International Commission of Jurist (ICJ) in 2014 as it limits appeals to states. The ICJ called on member states to not ratify the statute calling it "an empty gesture that will do nothing for the victims of human rights violations in the Middle East and North African (MENA) region" (International Commission of Jurist November 17, 2014, para. 1). In other words, the lack of appellate jurisdiction denies the individual victim of domestic human rights violations the ability to appeal outside the jurisdiction. The Organization of Islamic Conference (OIC) envisions an International Islamic Court of Justice (Romano 2013). Adopted in 1987, the court could adjudicate international dispute between member states based on Islamic *Shari'ah* or Islamic Law (Lombardini 2004).

In Latin America, Mercado Comum do Sul, or Common Market of the South (MERCOSUR also known as MERCOSUL or Ñemby Ñemuha[6]) was formed with the signing of the Treaty of Asuncion in 1991. It is primarily a trading block to improve relations among the member states as part of the process of integration by Argentina, Bolivia, Brazil, Paraguay, and Uruguay

(Venezuela was suspended indefinitely in 2016) along with associate members—Chile, Peru, Colombia, Guyana, Suriname, and Ecuador (Felter and Renwick December 26, 2017; Vervaele 2005). It is developing a framework for the MERCOSUR Court of Justice as part of further integration but has stopped short of creating an appellate court hearing appeals from domestic jurisdictions. Currently, the members support the MERCOSUR Dispute Resolution System which offers advisory opinions to the executive branches and domestic supreme courts of member states (Oliveira 2007). Further development of those regional forums is yet to unfold and deserves further study.

For the time being, the ECJ and ECtHR remain the most successful examples of modern extraterritorial courts. They have evolved over a long period of political peace among EU member states (Romano 2013) and are part of the growth of European law which is central to the broader process of European integration (Garrett, Kelemen and Schulz 1998). As the CCJ influences the growth and development of Caribbean jurisprudence, it is not unreasonable to project similar developments in other regional integration efforts. These developments exemplify the growing importance of extraterritorial courts around the world and the need to intensify and expand the research into their development, functions, and relationships with states.

NOTES

1. *Jabari Sensimania Nervais v The Queen* and *Dwayne Omar Severin v The Queen*. https://caribbeandeathpenaltyresearch.files.wordpress.com/2018/07/full-judgment-2018-ccj-19-aj.pdf.
2. *Boyce v the Queen* [2004] UKPC 32.
3. *August and Gabb v. The Queen* [2018] CCJ 7 (AJ).
4. *McEwan, Clarke, Fraser, Persaud and the Society against Sexual Orientation Discrimination (SASOD) vs. Attorney General of Guyana* (2018). ttp://ufdc.ufl.edu/AA00016900/00001.
5. *Orozco v. The Attorney General of Belize* (2016). http://www.u-rap.org/web2/images/Documents/Supreme-Court-Claim-No-668-of-2010-Caleb-Orozco-v-The-Attorney-General-of-Belize-et-al1.pdf.
6. "The Southern Common Market (MERCOSUR for its Spanish initials) is a regional integration process, initially established by Argentina, Brazil, Paraguay and Uruguay, and subsequently joined by Venezuela and Bolivia—the latter still complying with the accession procedure" (MECUSOR 2018).

Appendix A

The Length of Colonial Rule for Each State in the Sample (n = *50*)

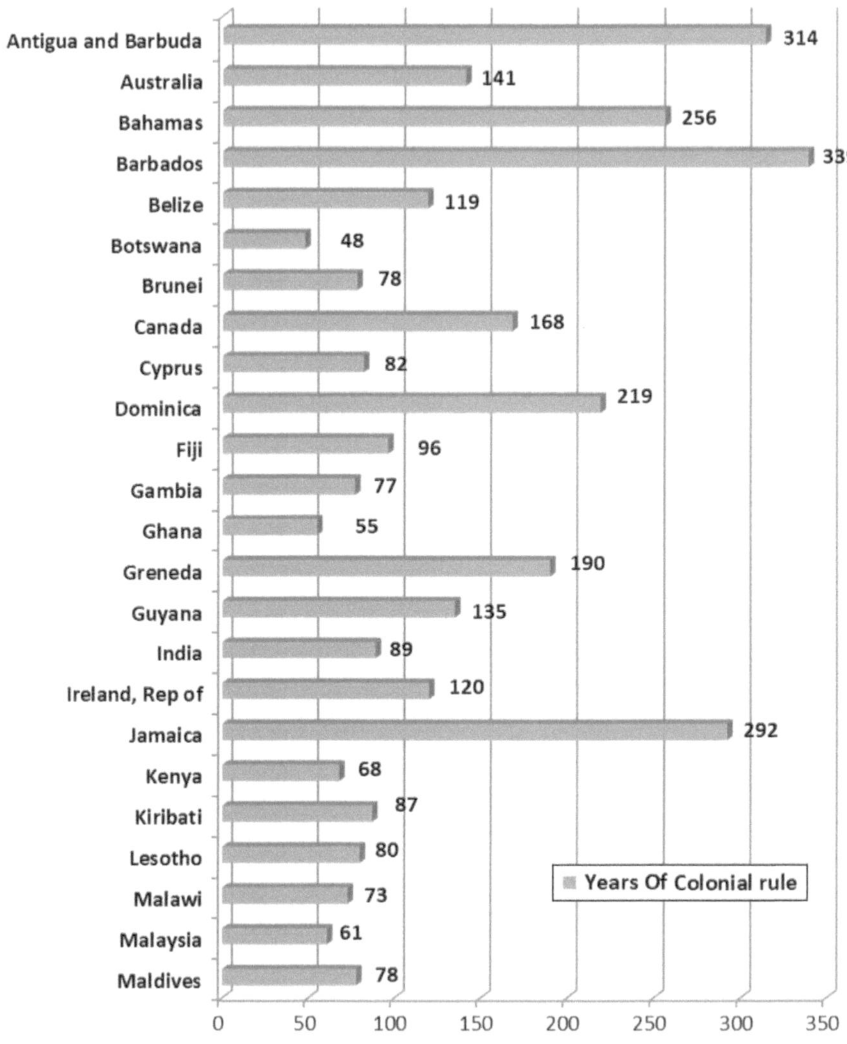

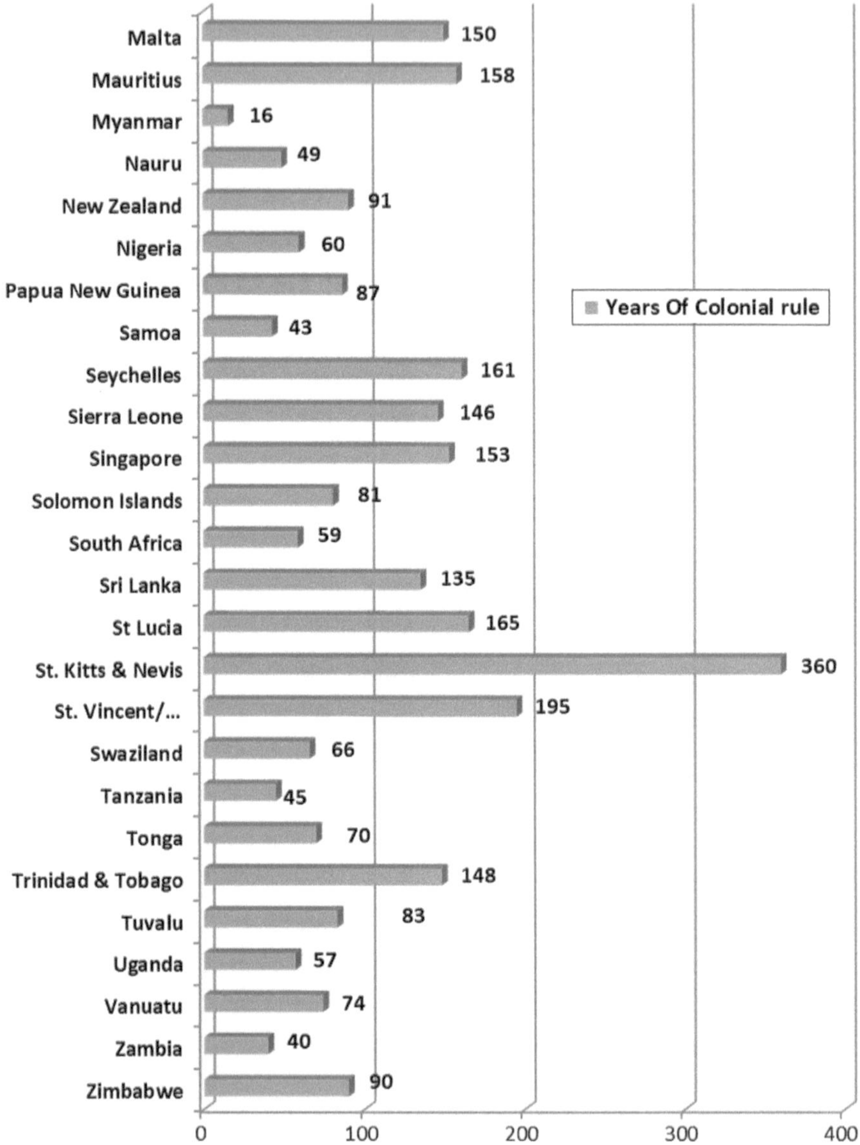
Malta 150
Mauritius 158
Myanmar 16
Nauru 49
New Zealand 91
Nigeria 60
Papua New Guinea 87
Samoa 43
Seychelles 161
Sierra Leone 146
Singapore 153
Solomon Islands 81
South Africa 59
Sri Lanka 135
St Lucia 165
St. Kitts & Nevis 360
St. Vincent/... 195
Swaziland 66
Tanzania 45
Tonga 70
Trinidad & Tobago 148
Tuvalu 83
Uganda 57
Vanuatu 74
Zambia 40
Zimbabwe 90
Years Of Colonial rule
0
100
200
300
400

Appendix B

The Fifty States, First Prime Ministers, whether Educated in the U.K. and Sources

Country	*Leader*	*U.K. Educated*	*Source*
Antigua/ Barbuda	Vere Bird	No	http://caribbeanheroes.com/index.php/30-the-right-doctor-honourable-vere-cornwall-bird-sr.html
Australia	Edmond Barton	No	http://www.britannica.com/EBchecked/topic/54441/Sir-Edmund-Barton
Belize	George Cadle Price	No	http://www.belize.com/george-price-belize.html
Canada	Richard Bedford Bennett	No	http://www.pc.gc.ca/APPS/CP-NR/release_e.asp?bgid=557&andor1=bg
Cyprus	Archbishop Makarios II	No	http://www.britannica.com/EBchecked/topic/359142/Makarios-III
Dominica	Patrick Roland John	No	http://thecommonwealth.org/our-member-countries/dominica/history http://www.lennoxhonychurch.com/heritage.cfm?Id=83
Fiji	Ratu Sir Kamisese Mara	No	http://www.britannica.com/EBchecked/topic/363718/Ratu-Sir-Kamisese-Mara
Ghana	Kwame Nkrumah	No	http://www.britannica.com/EBchecked/topic/416674/Kwame-Nkrumah
Grenada	Eric Matthew Gairy	No	http://www.britannica.com/EBchecked/topic/223562/Sir-Eric-Matthew-Gairy
Ireland, Rep of	William T. Cosgrave	No	http://www.britannica.com/EBchecked/topic/139138/William-Thomas-Cosgrave
Kenya	Jomo Kenyatta	No	http://www.britannica.com/EBchecked/topic/315185/Jomo-Kenyatta

(*Continued*)

Country	Leader	U.K. Educated	Source
Kiribati	Leremia Tabai	No	http://www.commonwealthofnations.org/commonwealth/eminent-persons-group/
Lesotho	Leabua Jonathon	No	http://www.encyclopedia.com/topic/Joseph_Leabua_Jonathan.aspx
Malawi	Hastings Kamuzu Banda	No	http://www.britannica.com/EBchecked/topic/51447/Hastings-Kamuzu-Banda
Maldives	Muhammad Fareed Didi	No	http://www.antimoon.com/forum/t14871.htm
Malta	Giorgio Borg Olivier	No	https://vassallohistory.wordpress.com/prime-minsters-of-malta/dr-giorgio-borg-olivier/
Myanmar	U Nu	No	http://www.britannica.com/EBchecked/topic/421460/U-Nu
Nauru	Maggabi DeRoburt	No	http://www.britannica.com/EBchecked/topic/158640/Hammer-DeRoburt
New Zealand	Joseph Ward	No	http://www.britannica.com/EBchecked/topic/635777/Sir-Joseph-Ward
Papua New Guinea	Michael Somare	No	http://www.polymernotes.org/biographies/PNG_bio_somare.htm
Samoa	Fiame Faumuina Mataafa	No	http://www.encyclopedia.com/topic/Samoa.aspx http://en.wikipedia.org/wiki/Fiame_Mata%27afa_Faumuina_Mulinu%27u_II
Solomon Islands	Peter Kenilorea	No	http://www.parliament.gov.sb/index.php?q=node/238
South Africa	Louis Botha	No	http://www.britannica.com/EBchecked/topic/75099/Louis-Botha
Sri Lanka	Don Stephen Senanayake	No	http://www.britannica.com/EBchecked/topic/534303/D-S-Senanayake
St. Kitts/Nevis	Kennedy Simmonds	No	http://historicbasseterre.com/hs_persons.asp?HSID=5&PID=11
Swaziland	King Sobhuza II	No	http://www.britannica.com/EBchecked/topic/550819/Sobhuza-II
Tuvalu	Toaripi Lauti	No	http://self.gutenberg.org/articles/toaripi_lauti
Tonga	Taufa'ahau Tupou IV	No	http://www.britannica.com/EBchecked/topic/1017392/Tupou-IV
Uganda	Milton Obote	No	http://www.britannica.com/EBchecked/topic/423934/Milton-Obote
Vanuatu	Father Walter Lini	No	http://www.britannica.com/EBchecked/topic/342449/the-Rev-Walter-Hayde-Lini
Zambia	Kenneth Kaunda	No	http://www.britannica.com/EBchecked/topic/313461/Kenneth-Kaunda
Zimbabwe	Robert Mugabe	No	http://www.britannica.com/EBchecked/topic/396102/Robert-Mugabe

(*Continued*)

Country	*Leader*	*U.K. Educated*	*Source*
Bahamas	Lynden Pindling	Yes	http://www.britannica.com/EBchecked/topic/460896/Sir-Lynden-Oscar-Pindling
Barbados	Grantley Adams	Yes	http://www.totallybarbados.com/barbados/About_Barbados/Local_Information/People/Barbados_Prime_Ministers/1st_Premier_of_Barbados_,045_Sir_Grantley_Herbert_Adams/
Botswana	Seretse Khama	Yes	http://www.britannica.com/EBchecked/topic/316195/Sir-Seretse-Khama
Brunei	Hassanal Bolkiah	Yes	http://www.britannica.com/EBchecked/topic/72165/Haji-Hassanal-Bolkiah-Muizzaddin-Waddaulah
Gambia	Dawda Kairaba Jawara	Yes	http://www.britannica.com/EBchecked/topic/301838/Sir-Dawda-Kairaba-Jawara
Guyana	Forbes Burnham	Yes	http://www.britannica.com/EBchecked/topic/85663/Forbes-Burnham
India	Jawaharlal Nehru	Yes	http://www.britannica.com/EBchecked/topic/408232/Jawaharlal-Nehru
Jamaica	Norman Manley	Yes	http://www.britannica.com/EBchecked/topic/362449/Norman-Manley
Malaysia	Tunku Abdul Rahman Putra Alhaj	Yes	http://www.britannica.com/EBchecked/topic/912/Tunku-Abdul-Rahman-Putra-Alhaj
Mauritius	Seewoosagur Ramgoolam	Yes	http://www.encyclopedia.com/doc/1G2-3435000151.html
Nigeria	Abubakar Tafawa Balewa	Yes	http://www.britannica.com/EBchecked/topic/50151/Sir-Abubakar-Tafawa-Balewa
Seychelles	James Richard Mancham	Yes	http://jamesmancham.com/biography.php
Sierra Leone	Milton Margai	Yes	http://www.britannica.com/EBchecked/topic/364553/Sir-Milton-Margai
Singapore	Lee Kuan Yew	Yes	http://www.britannica.com/EBchecked/topic/334621/Lee-Kuan-Yew
St. Lucia	John George Melvin Compton	Yes	http://archive.stlucia.gov.lc/primeminister/former_prime_ministers/john_g_m_compton/biography.htm
St. Vincent/Grenadines	Milton Cato	Yes	http://www.embsvg.com/History_of_SVG.htm http://self.gutenberg.org/articles/milton_cato
Tanzania/Zanzibar	Julius Nyerere	Yes	http://www.britannica.com/EBchecked/topic/423105/Julius-Nyerere
Trinidad/Tobago	Eric Williams	Yes	http://www.britannica.com/EBchecked/topic/644344/Eric-Williams

Bibliography

Acemuglo, Daron, Simon Johnson, and James A. Robinson. 2001. "The Colonial Origins of Comparative Development: An Empirical Investigation." *The American Economic Review* 91, no. 5: 1369–1401.

Acemuglo, Daron, Simon Johnson, and James A. Robinson. 2002. "Reversal of Fortune: Geography and Institutions in the Making of the Modern World Income Distribution." *The Quarterly Journal of Economics* 117, no. 4: 1231–1294.

African Court of Human and People's Rights. 2013. "Executive Council Twenty-Second Ordinary Session 21 – 25 January 2013 Addis Ababa, Ethiopia Report on The Activities of The African Court on Human and People's Rights." Accessed on October 10, 2015. http://www.african-court.org/en/index.php/publications/activity-reports/753-executive-council-twenty-second-ordinary-session-21-25-january-2013-addis-ababa-ethiopia-report-on-the-activities-of-the-african-court-on-human-and-people-s-rights.

African Court of Human and People's Rights. 2017. "Executive Council Thirtieth Ordinary Session 22 - 27 January 2017 Addis Ababa, Ethiopia, Report on The Activities of The African Court on Human and Peoples Rights." Accessed on October 10, 2015. http://www.african-court.org/en/index.php/publications/activity-reports/994-executive-council-thirtieth-ordinary-session-22-27-january-2017-addis-ababa-ethiopia-report-on-the-activities-of-the-african-court-on-human-and-peoples-rights.

African Court of Justice and Human Rights. n.d.a. *Jurisdiction: African Court of Justice and Human Rights.* Accessed on March 12, 2017. http://en.african-court.org/index.php/about-us/jurisdiction.

African Court of Justice and Human Rights. n.d.b. *Jurisdiction: Finalised Cases and Pending Cases. African Court of Justice and Human Rights.* Accessed on March 12, 2017. http://en.africancourt.org/index.php/13-homepage2/2-list-of-all-cases#finalised-cases.

African International Courts and Tribunals. n.d. *African Court of Justice.* Accessed on March 12, 2017. http://www.aict-ctia.org/courts_conti/acj/acj_home.html.

African Union. n.d. Judicial and Human Rights Institutions. *The African Court on Human and People's Rights*. Accessed on March 12, 2017. http://www.au.int/en/organs/cj.

Alemagung, Joy. 2010. "Post-Colonial Colonialism: An Analysis of International Factors and Actors Marring African Socio-economic and Political Development." *The Journal of Pan African Studies* 3, no. 10: 62–84.

Alphonse, Melanius. 2018. "CCJ Takes Centre Stage in Barbados Election." *Caribbean News Now*, May 20, 2018. https://wp.caribbeannewsnow.com/2018/05/20/ccj-takes-centre-stage-in-barbados-election/.

Amnesty International. 2016. "Death Penalty 2015: Facts and Figures." Accessed on February 23, 2017. https://www.amnesty.org/en/latest/news/2016/04/death-penalty-2015-facts-and-figures/.

Andic, Faut, Suphan Andic, and Doublas Dosser. 2011. *A Theory of Economic Integration for Developing Countries: Illustrated by Caribbean Countries*. New York and Oxen: Routledge.

Anthony, Kenny. 2003. "The Caribbean Court of Justice: Will It be a Hanging Court?" Accessed on April 19, 2017. https://archive.stlucia.gov.lc/primeminister/former_prime_ministers/kenny_d_anthony/statements/2003/the_caribbean_court_of_justice_will_it_be_a_hanging_court_june_28_2003.htm.

Atler, Karen J. 1998. "Who Are the 'Masters of the Treaty'? European Governments and the European Court of Justice." *International Organizations* 52, no. 1: 121–147.

BahamaCatholic. 2009. "Catholic Church Stands Firm against Death Penalty." Accessed on January 19, 2016. http://www.bahamacatholic.com/2009/10/catholic-church-remainsresolute-in-its.html.

Bailey, Michael, and Forrest Maltzman. 2008. "Does Legal Doctrine Matter? Unpacking Law and Policy Preferences on the Supreme Court." *American Political Science Review* 102, no. 3: 369–384.

Bartels, Brandon. 2003. "Advances in Duration Modeling: The Split Population Duration Model." Accessed on October 23, 2015. https://polisci.osu.edu/sites/polisci.osu.edu/files/AdvancesinDuration.pdf.

Baum, Lawrence. *American Courts Process and Policy*. Boston: Wadsworth, 2013.

BBC Caribbean. 2007. "Should the Caribbean Abolish the Death Penalty?" *BBC World News-Caribbean*, March 01, 2007. Accessed on June 26, 2015. http://www.bbc.co.uk/caribbean/news/story/2007/01/070112_tthanging.shtml.

BBC News. 2015. "1957: Malaya Celebrates Independence." Accessed on June 25, 2015. http://news.bbc.co.uk/onthisday/hi/dates/stories/august/31/newsid_3534000/3534340.stm.

Bernhard, Michael. 2015. "Chronic Instability and the Limits of Path Dependency." *Perspectives in Politics* 13, no. 4: 976–991.

Beth, Loren P. 1977. "The Judicial Committee of the Privy Council and the Development of Judicial Review." *The American Journal of Comparative Law* 24, no. 1: 22–42.

Bickel, Alexander M. 1962. *The Least Dangerous Branch. Indianapolis.* Indiana: Bobbs-Merrill.

Blackstone Chambers. 2016. "Criminalisation of Homosexuality Declared Unconstitutional." *Blackstone Chambers*, August 11, 2016. https://www.blackstonechambers.com/news/orozco-v-attorney-general-belize/.

Borland, Orlando Nigel. 1977. *The Formation of a Colonial Society: Belize, from Conquest to Crown Colony*. Hull: University of Hull.

Bowcott, Owen. "Senior UN Official Warns against UK Plans to Scrap Human Rights Act." *The Guardian*, October 12, 2015. Accessed on January 6, 2016. http://www.theguardian.com/law/2015/oct/12/un-official-warns-against-uk-plans-scrap-human-rights-act.

Box-Steffensmeier, Janet M., and Bradford S. Jones. 2004. *Event History Modeling: A Guide for Social Scientists*. Cambridge: Cambridge University Press.

Box-Steffensmeier, Janet M., and Christopher J.W. Zorn. 2001. "Duration Models and Proportional Hazards in Political Science." *American Journal of Political Science* 45, no. 4: 972–988.

British and Irish Legal Information Institute. 2014. "The Judicial Committee of the Privy Council Decisions." Accessed on July 7, 2015. http://www.bailii.org/uk/cases/UKPC/.

Brown, Christopher. 2002. *Sovereignty, Rights and Justice*. Cambridge: Polity Press.

Burnham, Margaret A. 2005. "Indigenous Constitutionalism and The Death Penalty: The Case of the Commonwealth Caribbean." *International Journal of Constitutional Law* 3, no. 4: 582–616.

Burns, Peter T. 1984. "The Judicial Committee of the Privy Council: Constitutional Bulwark or Colonial Remnant?" *Otago Law* 5: 503–522.

Capoccia, Giovanni, and R. Daniel Kelmen. 2002. "The Study of Critical Junctures: Theory, Narrative, and Counterfactuals in Historical Institutionalism." *World Politics* 59, no. 3: 341–369.

Caribbean Community Secretariat. 2001. "The Agreement Establishing the CCJ, The Caribbean Court of Justice." Accessed on July 3, 2017. http://www.caribbeancourtofjustice.org/wp-content/uploads/2011/09/ccj_agreement.pdf.

Caribbean Community Secretariat. 2011. "History of Caribbean Community." Accessed on July 3, 2017. http://www.caricom.org/jsp/community/history.jsp?menu=community.

Caribbean Court of Justice. 2012. "CCJ Trust Fund." Accessed on July 5, 2017. http://www.ccj.org/about-the-ccj/ccj-trust-fund.

Caribbean Court of Justice. 2017. "Appellate Jurisdiction Judgments." Accessed on July 5, 2017. http://www.ccj.org/judgments-proceedings/appellate-jurisdiction-judgments.

Caribbean News Now. 2004. "Privy Council to Rule on Caribbean Death Penalty." Accessed on July 3, 2017. http://www.caribbeannewsnow.com/caribnet/2004/03/23/penalty.htm.

Caribbean360. 2017. "CARIBBEAN: Trinidad President Urges Region to Dump Privy Council." *St. Lucia News Online*, August 25, 2017. Accessed on November 3, 2017. https://www.stlucianewsonline.com/caribbean-trinidad-president-urges-region-to-dump-privy-council/.

CARICOM. 2001. "Revised Treaty of Chaguaramas Establishing the Caribbean Community Including the CARICOM Single Market and Economy." Accessed on April 4, 2017. https://caricom.org/documents/4906-revised_treaty-text.pdf.

CARICOM. 2001. "The West Indies Federation." Accessed on April 14, 2017. https://caricom.org/community/the-west-indies-federation/#.

CARICOM. 2018. "Who We Are: Pillars of Integration." Accessed on April 14, 2017. https://caricom.org/about-caricom/who-we-are.

CARICOM. n.d. "Who We Are: Pillars of Integration." Accessed on April 9, 2015. https://caricom.org/about-caricom/who-we-are.

Carson, Jamie L., and Benjamin A. Kleinerman. 2002. "A Switch in Time Saves Nine: Institutions, Strategic Actors and FDR's Court-packing Plan." *Public Choice* 113, no. 3: 301–324.

Casper, Jonathan D. 1976. "The Supreme Court and National Policy-Making." *American Political Science Review* 70, no. 1: 50–63.

Chayes, Abram, and Anne-Marie Slaughter. 2000. "The ICC and the Future of the Global Legal System." In *National Security and International Law: The United States and the International Criminal Court*, edited by Sarah B. Sewall and Carl Kaysen, 237–247. Lanham: Rowman & Littlefield Publishers, Inc.

CMC. 2018. "Grenada PM Wants to Re-Open Dialogue on CCJ." *St. Lucia News Online*, March 26, 2018. https://www.stlucianewsonline.com/grenada-pm-wants-to-re-open-dialogue-on-ccj/.

Collet, Dave. 1994. *Modeling Survival Data in Medical Research*. London: Chapman and Hall.

"Committee of the Privy Council." In *Power in History: From Medieval to the Post-Modern World*, edited by Anthony McElligott, et al. Newbridge: Irish Academic Press.

Commonwealth Network. 2015. Commonwealth Member Countries: South Africa. Accessed on July 30, 2015. http://www.commonwealthofnations.org/yb-pdfs/south_africa_country_profile.pdf.

Cooper, Phillip J. 1985. "Conflict or Constructive Tension: The Changing Relationship of Judges and Administrators." *Public Administration Review* 45: 643–652.

Corley, Pamela C, Amy Steigerwalt, and Artemus Ward. 2013. *The Puzzle of Unanimity: Consensus on the United States Supreme Court*. Stanford: Stanford University Press.

Cox, Noel. 2002. "The Abolition or Retention of the Privy Council as the Final Court of Appeal for New Zealand: Conflict between National Identity and Legal Pragmatism." *New Zealand Law Review* 20, no. 2: 220–238.

Crosby, Alfred. 1986. *Ecological Imperialism: The Biological Expansion of Europe 900-1900*. New York: Cambridge University Press.

Crouch, Colin, and Henry Farrell. 2004. "Breaking the Path of Institutional Development? Alternatives to the New Determinism." *Rationality and Society* 16, no. 1: 5–43.

Currie, David P. 1987. "The Constitution in the Supreme Court: The New Deal, 1931-1940." *University of Chicago Law Review* 54, no. 2: 504–555.

Dahl, Robert A. 1957. "Decision-Making in a Democracy: The Supreme Court as a National Policy-Maker." *Journal of Public Law* 6: 279–291.

Das, Tirthankar. 2007. "Performance of the Indian Supreme Court during the Emergency." Accessed on March 23, 2017. http://works.bepress.com/cgi/viewcontent.cgi?article=1001&context=tirthankar_das.

DataBanks International. 2015a. "Cross-National Time Series Data Archive." Accessed on December 21, 2015. http://www.databanksinternational.com/.

DataBanks International. 2015b. "Domestic Conflict Event Data Definitions." Accessed on December 21, 2015. http://www.cntsdata.com/#!domconflict/c1svs.

Davenport, Christian. 1995. "Multi-Dimensional Threat Perception and State Repression: An Inquiry into Ways States Apply Negative Sanctions." *American Journal of Political Science* 39, no. 3: 683–713.

De Brujn, Jurriën. 2014. "The Role of Regime Types on Bilateral Trade Levels." Accessed on August 29, 2015. https://pdfs.semanticscholar.org/e26d/b03fb7ffb32617359c89b0ff40289dce0ddc.pdf?_ga=2.229080724.949420557.1577147658-800039625.1577147658.

De, Rohit. 2012. "Emasculating the Executive: The Federal Court and Civil Liberties in Late Colonial India, 1943-1944." In *Fates of Political Liberalism in British Post-Colony: The Politics of Legal Complex*, edited by Terence C. Halliday, Lucien Kovpik, and Malcolm Feeley, 59–90. New York: Cambridge University Press.

Death Penalty Information Center. 2018. "Abolitionist and Retentionist Countries." Accessed on April 2, 2018. https://deathpenaltyinfo.org/abolitionist-and-retentionist-countries.

Delgado, Richard. 2008. "A Comment on Rosenberg's New Edition of the Hollow Hope." *Northwestern University Law Review* (Colloquy 103). Accessed on September 7, 2015. http://scholarlycommons.law.northwestern.edu/cgi/viewcontent.cgi?article=1137&context=nulr_online.

Diop, Samba. 2012. "African Elites and their Post-Colonial Legacy: Cultural, Political and Economic Discontent." *Africa Development* 37, no. 4: 221–235.

Dippel, Christian, and Jean Paul Carvalho. 2014. "The Iron Law of Oligarchy: The Post-Slavery Caribbean Sugar Colonies." Accessed on April 17, 2017. http://eh.net/eha/wp-content/uploads/2015/05/Dippel.pdf.

Djelic, Marie-Laure, and Segrid Quack. 2007. "Overcoming Path Dependency: Path Generation in Open Systems." *Theory and Society* 36, no. 2: 161–186.

Dorney, John. (2012). "The Irish War of Independence- A Brief Overview." *The Irish Story*. Accessed on April 2, 2018. http://www.theirishstory.com/2012/09/18/the-irish-war-of-independencea-brief-overview/#.Vg3oKvlVikp.

Doyle, Michael W. 1986. *Empires*. Ithaca: Cornel University Press.

Du Plessis, Max, Tiyanjana Maluwa, and Annie O'Reilly. 2013. "African and International Criminal Court." *Chatham House*. https://www.chathamhouse.org/sites/files/chathamhouse/public/Research/International%20Law/0713pp_iccafrica.pdf.

Duggard, John. 2013. "Palestine and the International Criminal Court: Institutional Failure or Bias?" *Journal of International Criminal Justice* 11, no. 3: 563–570.

Eckstein, Harry, and Robert H. Gurr. 1975. *Patterns of Authority: A Structural Basis for Political Inquiry*. New York: Wiley-Interscience.

Elden, Stuart. 2006. "Contingent Sovereignty, Territorial Integrity and the Sanctity of Borders." *SAIS Review of International Affairs* 29: 11–24.

Elgot, Jessica. 2015. "British Judges Not Bound by European Court of Human Rights, says Levenson." *The Guardian*, May 15, 2015. Accessed on June 11, 2018. http://www.theguardian.com/law/2015/may/24/british-courts-echr-leveson.

Encyclopedia Britannica. 2015. *East India Company*. Accessed on October 12, 2015. http://www.britannica.com/topic/East-India-Company.

Epstein, Lee, and Thomas G. Walker. 2014. *Constitutional Law for a Changing America: A Short Course.* Washington DC: CQ Press.

Feeley, Malcolm M., and Edward L. Rubin. 1999. *Judicial Policy-making and the Modern State: How the Courts Reformed America's Prisons.* Cambridge: Cambridge University Press.

Felter, Claire, and Danielle Renwick. 2017. "Mercosur: South America's Fractious Trade Bloc." *Council on Foreign Relations*. Accessed on August 27, 2016. https://www.cfr.org/backgrounder/mercosur-south-americas-fractious-trade-bloc.

Fenno, Richard F. 1986. "Observation, Context and Sequence in the Study of Political Science." *American Political Science Review* 80, no. 1: 3–15.

Ferguson, Niall. 2003. *Empire: How Britain Made the Modern World.* London: Penguin Books.

Fieldhouse, David K. 2006. *Western Imperialism in the Middle East 1914–1958*. New York: Oxford University Press.

Finlay, Bryan, and Frank E. Walwyn. 2008. "Such as They are, They are Our Own: A Talk on Abolishing Canadian Appeals to the Privy Council." Accessed on November 24, 2016. http://www.eccourts.org/static/jei_doc/2008/book_launch/ATalkonAbolishingCanadianAp pealstothePrivyCouncilbyBryanFinlayandFrankWalwyn.pdf.

Fisher, Michael H. 1991. *Indirect Rule in India: Residents and Residency Systems, 1776-1858*. Delhi: Oxford University Press.

Fraser, Tony. n.d. "Jamaica, Trinidad and the CCJ." *Caribbean Intelligence*. Accessed on May 23, 2017. https://www.caribbeanintelligence.com/content/jamaica-trinidad-and-ccj.

Freedom House. 2014a. "Freedom in the World 2014: The Annual Survey of Political Rights and Civil Liberties-Individual Country Ratings and Status." *Washington (1972-2014)*. Accessed on May 2, 2015. Retrieved from https://freedomhouse.org/report-types/freedom-world#.VWxNS89VhBc.

Freedom House. 2014a. "Freedom in the World 2014: The Annual Survey of Political Rights and Civil Liberties-Individual Country Ratings and Status." *Washington (1972-2014)*. Accessed on September 2, 2016. https://freedomhouse.org/report-types/freedom-world#.VWxNS89VhBc.

Freedom House. 2014b. "Freedom in the World Methodology." Accessed on April 3, 2015. https://www.freedomhouse.org/report/freedom-world-2014/methodology#.VZlJ5vlVhBd.

Frymer, Paul. 2003. "Acting when Elected Official Won't: Federal Courts and Civil Rights Enforcement in U.S. Labor Unions, 1935-1985." *American Political Science Review* 97, no. 3: 843–858.

Gad, S.C. 2010. "Statistical Methods in Toxicology." In *Comprehensive Toxicology*, edited by Charlene A. McQueen, 183–197. Oxford: Elsevier.

Gadbois, George H. 1963. "Program in Comparative Studies on Southern Asia: Evolution of the Federal Court of India: An Historical Footnote." *Journal of the Indian Law Institute* 5: 19–45.

Galligan, Denis, and Mila Versteeg. 2013. *Social and Political Foundations of Constitutions*. New York: Cambridge University Press.

Garrett, Geoffrey, Daniel Kelemen, and Heiner Schulz. 1998. "The European Court of Justice, National Governments and Legal Integration in the European Union." *International Organization* 52, no. 9: 149–176.

Gerring, John. Daniel Ziblatt, Johann Van Gorp, and Julian Arevalo. 2011. "An Institutional Theory of Direct and Indirect Rule." *World Politics* 63, no. 3: 377–433.

Geyh, Charles Gardner. 2006. "Why Courts & Congress Collide and Why their Conflicts Subside." *The American Bar Association*. Accessed on November 27, 2016. http://apps.americanbar.org/publiced/constitutionday/WhyCourtsCongress Collide.pdf.

Ghai, Yash, and Guido Galli. 2007. "Constitution-Building Processes and Democratization: Lessons Learned." *International IDEA*. Accessed on January 29, 2017. http://www.idea.int/publications/dchs/upload/dchs_vol2_sec6_2.pdf.

Ghany, Hamid A. 2000. "The Death Penalty, Human Rights and British Law Lords: Judicial Opinion on Delay of Execution in the Commonwealth Caribbean." *International Journal of Human Rights* 4, Issue 2: 30–43.

Girvan, Norman. 2001. *Reinterpreting the Caribbean in New Caribbean Thought: A Reader*. Jamaica: University of West Indies Press.

Goel, M.K., P. Khanna, and J. Kishore. 2010. "Understanding Survival Analysis: Kaplan-Meier Estimate." *International Journal of Ayurveda Research* 1, no. 4: 274–278.

Golani, Motti. 2009. *The End of the British Mandate for Palestine, 1948: The Diary of Sir Henry Gurney*. New York: Palgrave Macmillan.

Gordon, Donald L. 2007. "African Politics." In *Understanding Contemporary Africa*, edited by April A. Gordon and Donald L. Gordon, 61–114. Boulder: Lynne Rienner.

Gott, Richard. 2011. *Britain's Empire: Resistance, Repression and Revolt*. London: Verso.

Grier, R.M. 1999. "Colonial Legacies and Economic Growth." *Public Choice* 98: 317–335.

Hansard. Ghana (Consequential Provision) Bill. House of Lords Debate, Volume 623 (May 30, 1960), Column (s) 92–992. Accessed on February 24, 2018. https://hansard.parliament.uk/Commons/1960-05-17/debates/af24a57e-b5dd-4426-bc88-722325a5f25b/Ghana(ConsequentialProvision)Bill.

Harrington, Joanna. 2004. "The Challenge to the Mandatory Death Penalty in the Commonwealth Caribbean." *The American Journal of International Law* 98, no. 1: 126–140.

Harvey, William Bennett. 1962. "The Evolution of Ghana Law since Independence: Law and Contemporary Problems." *African Law* 27: 581–604.

Haslam J. 1972. "The Judicial Committee—Past Influence and Future Relationships." *The New Zealand Law Journal*: 542–555.

Hauss, Charles. 2015. *Comparative Politics: Domestic Responses to Global Challenges*. Stamford: Cengage Learning.

Heifer, Laurence R. 2002. "Overlegalizing Human Rights: International Relations Theory and the Commonwealth Caribbean Backlash against Human Rights Regimes." *Columbia Law Review* 102: 1832–1911.

Henley, Jon. 2013. "Why Is the European Court of Human Rights Hated by the UK Right?" *The Guardian,* December 22, 2013. Accessed on June 18, 2015. http://www.theguardian.com/law/2013/dec/22/britain-european-court-human-rights.

Hirari, Jacob Gerner. 2012. "The Autocratic Legacy of Early Statehood." *American Political Science Review* 106, no. 3: 471–494.

Hirschl, Ran. 2000. "The Political Origins of Judicial Empowerment through Constitutionalism: Lessons from Four Constitutional Revolutions." *Law & Social Inquiry* 25, no. 1: 91–149.

Hogg, Michael. 2006. "Social Identity Theory." In *Contemporary Social Psychological Theories*, edited by P.J. Burke, 111–136. Palo Alto: Stanford University Press.

Hönnige, Christopher. 2011. "Beyond Judicialization: Why We Need More Comparative Research about Constitutional Courts." *European Political Science* 10: 346–358.

Hooker, M.B. 1975. *Legal Pluralism: An Introduction to Colonial and Neo-Colonial Laws.* Oxford: Clarendon Press.

Howard, Robert M., and Amy Steigerwalt. 2012. *Judging Law and Policy: Courts and Policy Making in the American Political System.* New York and London: Routledge.

Howell, P.A. 1979. *The Judicial Committee of the Privy Council 1833-1876: It's Origins, Structure and Development*. New York: Cambridge University Press.

Huntington, Samuel P. 1991. *Third Wave: Democratization in the Late Twentieth Century.* Norman: University of Oklahoma Press.

Hyam, Ronald, and Peter Henslaw. 2003. *The Lion and the Springbok: Britain and South Africa since the Boer War*. Cambridge: Cambridge University Press.

Ibhawoh, Bonny. 2013. "Asserting Judicial Sovereignty: The Debate over the Abolition of Privy Council Jurisdiction in British Africa." In *Legal Histories of the British Empire: Laws, Engagements and Legacies*, edited by Shaunnagh Dorsett and John McLaren. New York: Routledge.

International Commission of Jurists. 2014. "Arab League's Human Rights Court Will Not Bring Justice to Victims of Violations." Accessed on June 28, 2017. https://www.icj.org/arab-leagues-human-rights-court-will-not-bring-justice-to-victims-of-violations/.

International Commission of Jurists. 2016. "Belize Scraps Law Targeting Gay Men." Accessed on June 28, 2017. http://www.humandignitytrust.org/pages/NEWS/Press%20Releases?NewsArticleID=51.

International Court of Justice. "Jurisdiction." Accessed on October 23, 2015. https://www.icj-cij.org/en/jurisdiction.

International Criminal Court. 2015a. "About the Court." Accessed on October 23, 2015. https://www.icc-cpi.int/about.

International Criminal Court. 2015b. "ICC at a Glance." Accessed on December 12, 2015. https://www.icc-cpi.int/Publications/ICCAtAGlanceENG.pdf.

International Criminal Court. 2015c. "Cases." Accessed on December 12, 2015. https://www.icc-cpi.int/cases.

International Monetary Fund. 2013. "World Economic Outlook Database." Accessed on April 12, 2017. https://www.imf.org/external/pubs/ft/weo/2013/02/weodata/index.aspx.

Iweriebor, Ehiedu E.G. 2011. "The Colonization of Africa." Accessed on March 17, 2017. http://exhibitions.nypl.org/africanaage/essay-colonization-of-africa.html.

Iyer, Lakshmi. 2010. "Direct Versus Indirect Colonial Rule in India: Long Term Consequences." *The Review of Economics and Statistics* 92, no. 4: 693–713.

Jain, M.P. 2014. *Indian Legal History 2006*. Morrisville: Lulu Press.

Jammeh, Ousman A.S. 2011. *The Constitutional Law of the Gambia: 1965-2010*. Bloomington: Authorhouse.

Jenkins, Stephen. 2001. "A Discrete-time Split Population Survival ('cure') Model for Stata 6 or Stata 7: spsurv. Presentation UK Stata User Group Meeting," May 15, 2001. Accessed on March 17, 2015. https://www.iser.essex.ac.uk/files/teaching/stephenj/ec968/pdfs/UKSUG7-spsurv.pdf.

Joseph, Phillip. 1985. "Towards Abolition of the Privy Council Appeals: The Judicial Committee and the Bill of Rights." *Canterbury Law Review* 2: 273–297.

Judd, C.M., G.H. McClelland, and C.S. Ryan. 2009. *Data Analysis: A Model Comparison Approach*. New York: Routledge/Taylor & Francis Group.

Judicial Committee of the Privy Council. 2015. *The Judicial Committee*. Accessed on March 17, 2018. https://www.jcpc.uk/about/judicial-committe.html.

Juegensmeyer, Julian Conrad. 1964. "African Presidentialism: A Comparison of the "Executive" under the Constitutions of the Federation of Nigeria, the Federal Republics of the Congo and Cameroon, and the Republics of Ghana, Chad, Congo and the Entente." *Journal of African Law* 8, no. 3: 157–177.

Justia. n.d. "U.S. Law. Acts of Congress Held Unconstitutional in Whole or in Part by the Supreme Court of the United States." Accessed on February 15, 2017. https://law.justia.com/constitution/us/046-acts-of-congress-held-unconstitutional.html.

Justice at Stake Campaign. "Justice at Stake Frequency Questionnaire." *Greenberg, Quinlan, and Rosner Research Institute*. Accessed on June 2, 2017. http://www.justiceatstake.org/media/cms/JASNationalSurveyResults_6F537F99272D4.pdf.

Katende, J.W., and George W. Kanyeihamba. 1973. "Legalism and Politics in East Africa: The Dilemma of the East African Court of Appeal for East Africa." *Transition* 43: 43–54.

Kawa. 2016. "Collapse of the East African Community." *African Nationalism and New States in Africa* (blog). January 10, 2016. http://kawanationalism.blogspot.com/2016/01/collapse-of-east-african-community.html.

Keck, Thomas M. 2007. "Party, Policy, or Duty: Why Does the Supreme Court Invalidate Federal Statutes?" *American Political Science Review* 101, no. 3: 321–338.

Keith Camp, Linda, and Ayo Ogundele. 2007. "Legal Systems and Constitutionalism in Sub-Saharan Africa: An Empirical Examination of Colonial Influences on Human Rights." *Human Rights Quarterly* 29: 1065–1097.

Kelly, Maurice. 1994. "Leaving Their Lordships: The Commonwealth Experience." *The New Zealand Law Journal*: 101–109.

Kerr, Roger. 2002. "Abolition of Privy Council Major Constitutional Issue, New Zealand Business Round Table, December 10, 2002." Accessed on November 16, 2015. http://www.nzbr.org.nz/documents/releases/releases-2002/abolition_appeals.doc.htm.

Kirby, Michael. 2008. *The Lords, Tom Bingham and Australia*. Accessed on January 21, 2017. http://www.hcourt.gov.au/assets/publications/speeches/formerjustices/kirbyj/kirbyj_mar08.pdf.

Klarman, Michael. 2004. *From Jim Crow to Civil rights: The Supreme Court and the Struggle for Racial Equality*. New York: Oxford University Press.

Kohli, Atul. 1994. "Where do High Growth Political Economies Come from? The Japanese Lineage of Korea's 'Developmental State'." *World Development* 22, no. 9: 1269–1293.

Lange, Mathew. 2004. "British Colonial Legacies and Political Development." *World Development* 32, no. 6: 905–922.

Lange, Mathew. 2009. *Lineages of Despotism and Development: British Colonialism and State Power*. Chicago and London: University of Chicago Press.

Lawrence, James. 1996. *The Rise and Fall of the British Empire*. New York: Macmillan 1996.

Linz, Juan J. 1975. "Totalitarian and Authoritarian Regimes: Handbook of Political Science." In *Macropolitical Theory Volume 3*, edited by F.L. Greenstein and N.W. Polsby, 175–412. Reading: Addison Wesley.

Linz, Juan J. 2000. *Totalitarian and Authoritarian Regimes*. Boulder: Lynne Reinner Publishers.

Lombardini, Michelle. 2004. "The International Islamic Court of Justice: Towards an International Islamic Legal System?" *Leiden Journal of International Law* 14, no. 3: 665–680.

Long, J. Scott. 1997. *Regression Models for Categorical and Limited Dependent Variables*. Thousand Oaks: Sage Publications.

Lupo, Yonaton, and Erik Voeten. 2001. "The Role of Precedent at the European Court of Human Rights: A Network Analysis of Case Citations." *British Journal of Political Science* 42, no. 2: 413–429.

Mahoney, James. 2000. "Path Dependence in Historical Sociology." *Theory and Society* 29, no. 4: 507–548.

Malleson, Kate. 1999. *The New Judiciary: The Effects of Expansion and Activism*. Aldershot: Dartmouth Publishing Company, Ltd.

Mamdani, Mahmood. 1996. *Citizen and Subject: Contemporary Africa and the Legacy of Late Colonialism*. Princeton: Princeton University Press.

Mamdani, Mahmood. 1999. "Historicizing Power and Responses to Power: Indirect Rule and its Reform." *Social Research* 66, no. 3: 859–886.

Manifesto '07. 2007. "A Matter of Trust." Accessed on November 28, 2015. http://www.caribbeanelections.com/eDocs/manifestos/bs/FNM_Manifesto_2007.pdf.

Mann, Michael. 1984. "The Autonomous Power of the State: Its Origins, Mechanism and Results." *European Journal of Sociology* 25, Issue 02: 185–213.

Mapsofindia. 2015. *Flag*. Accessed on February 20, 2015. http://www.mapsofindia.com/maps/india/nationalflag.htm.

Markovitz, Irving L. 1987. *Studies in Power and Class in Africa*. Oxford: Oxford University Press.

Mather, Lynn. 1995. "The Fired Football Coach (Or, How Trial Courts Make Policy)." In *Contemplating Courts*, edited by Lee Epstein, 170–220. Washington DC: Congressional Quarterly Press.

Maxwell School of Citizenship and Public Affairs. 2005. "Maxwell Poll on Civic Engagement and Inequality." *Campbell Public Affairs Institute*. Accessed on June 23, 2017. http://www.maxwell.syr.edu/uploadedFiles/campbell/data_sources/Law%20and%20Court s%20Questions%20from%202005%20Poll.pdf.

McCann, Michael W. 1986. *Taking Reform Seriously: Perspectives on Public Interest Liberalism*. Ithaca: Cornel University Press.

McCartney, Mathew. 2015. *Economic Growth and Development: A Comparative Introduction*. London: Palgrave.

McKeever, Robert J. 1997. *The United States Supreme Court: A Political and Legal Analysis*. Manchester and New York: Manchester University Press.

Melnick, R. Shep. 1994. "The Policies of Partnerships." *Public Administration Review* 45: 653–660.

MERCUSOR. 2018. "What Is MERCOSUR?" *MERCUSOR in Brief*. Accessed on December 27, 2019. https://www.mercosur.int/en/about-mercosur/mercosur-in-brief/.

Meredeth, Martin. 2005. *The Fate of Africa: From the Hopes of Freedom to the Heart of Despair: A History of Fifty Years of Independence*. New York: Public Affairs.

Merriam-Webster. 2015a. *Dictionary*. Accessed on November 22, 2018. http://www.merriamwebster.com/dictionary/curia%20regis.

Mills, Therese. 2005. "Letter: Colonial Power over Death Penalty." *BBC News*, January 19, 2005. Accessed on December 18, 2015. http://news.bbc.co.uk/2/hi/americas/4185745.stm.

Minnis, Hubert A. 2014. "New Year's Address by Opposition Leader, Hon. Dr. Hubert A. Minnis." *Bahamas Island Info*. Accessed on February 22, 2016. http://www.bahamaislandsinfo.com/index.php?option=com_content&view=article&id=16777:2014-new-years-address-by-opposition-leader-hon-dr-hubert-minnis&catid=34:Bahamas%20National%20News&Itemid=147.

Mitchell, Sara McLaughlin, Jonathan J. Ring, and May K. Spellman. 2013. "Domestic Legal Traditions and States' Human Rights Practices." *Journal of Peace Research* 50, no. 2: 189–202.

Mohr, Thomas. 2010. "'A British Empire Court'—A Brief Appraisal of the History of the Judicial Committee of the Privy Council". *UCD Working Papers in Law, Criminology & Socio-Legal Studies Research Paper No. 30/2010*. Accessed on June 13, 2015. http://dx.doi.org/10.2139/ssrn.1638897.

Moralski, Bryon J., and Charles R. Shipan. 1999. "The Politics of Supreme Court Nominations: A Theory of Institutional Constraints and Choices." *American Journal of Political Science* 43, no. 4: 1069–1095.

Mwakikagile, Godfrey. *British Honduras to Belize: Transformation of a Nation*. Dar es Salaam: New Africa Press 2014.

Mwalimu, Robert. 2007. *The Nigerian Legal System, Volume 1: Public Law*. New York: Peter Lang Publishing.

Nations Online Project. 2015. "Least Developed Countries." Accessed on April 2, 2017. http://www.nationsonline.org/oneworld/least_developed_countries.htm.

O'Conner, Sharon Hamby, and Mary Sarah Bilder. 2012. "Appeals to the Privy Council before American Independence: An Annotated Digital Catalogue. Legal Studies Research Paper Series. Boston College Law School." *Law Library Journal* 104, no. 1: 83–97.

O'Donnell, Guillermo. 1973. *Bureaucratic Authoritarianism: Argentina 1966-1973.* Berkeley: University of California Press

Oliveira, Maria Ângela Jardim de Santa Cruz. 2007. "Judicial Diplomacy: The Role of the Supreme Courts in Mercosur Legal Integration." *Harvard International Law Journal* 48: 93–100. http://www.harvardilj.org/wp-content/uploads/2011/05/HILJ-Online_48_Oliveira.pdf.

Organization of American States. 2011. *Inter-American Commission on Human Rights.* Accessed on January 31, 2016. http://www.oas.org/en/iachr/mandate/what.asp.

Page, Scott E. 2006. "Path Dependence." *Quarterly Journal of Political Science* 1, no. 1: 87–115.

Pearson, Allison. 2015. "We Must Get Rid of the Dreadful Human Rights Act." *The Telegraph,* May 13, 2015. Accessed on May 28, 2018. http://www.telegraph.co.uk/news/uknews/law-and-order/11602222/Allison-Pearson-We-must-get-rid-of-the-dreadful-Human-Rights-Act.html#article.

Pierson, Paul. 2004. *Politics in Time: History, Institutions, and Social Analysis.* Princeton: Princeton University Press.

Polity IV Project. 2013. "Political Regime Characteristics and Transitions, 1800-2013." *Center for Systemic Peace.* Accessed on September 22, 2018. http://systemicpeace.org/polity/polity4.htm.

Polity IV Project: Dataset User's Manual. 2013. *Center for Systemic Peace.* Accessed on September 22, 2018. http://www.systemicpeace.org/inscr/p4manualv2012.pdf.

Populstat. 2006a. *United Kingdom.* Accessed on September 12, 2015. http://www.populstat.info/Europe/unkingdc.htm.

Populstat. 2006b. *India.* Accessed on October 2, 2015. http://www.populstat.info/Asia/indiac.htm.

Porter, Andrew. 1999. "The Oxford History of the British Empire: Volume III: The Nineteenth Century." In *The Oxford History of The British Empire.* New York, Oxford University Press.

Porter, Bernard. 2012. "Cutting the British Empire Down to Size." *History Today,* October 10, 2012. Accessed on April 15, 2015. http://www.historytoday.com/bernard-porter/cutting-british-empiredown-size.

Pramdas, Ralph. 1996. "Ethnicity and Identity in the Caribbean: Decentering a Myth." *The Helen Kellogg Institute for International Studies.* Accessed on July 5, 2016. http://nd.edu/~kellogg/publications/workingpapers/WPS/234.pdf.

Prasad, T. 2011. "Independence Day of India—A Retrospective." *Gandhitopia,* August 18, 2011. Accessed on July 19, 2018. http://www.gandhitopia.org/profiles/blogs/independence-day-of-india-a-retrospection.

Privy Council. n.d. "Overview". Accessed on April 10, 2017. http://privycouncil.independent.gov.uk/privycouncil/.

Rao, Prasada, and Eliyathamby Selvanathan. 1990. "A Method for Computation of Stand Errors for Geary-Khamis Parties and International Prices." Accessed on May 13, 2015. http://www.researchgate.net/profile/DS_Rao/publication/265980465_A_METHOD_FOR_THE_COMPUTATION_OF_STANDARD_ERRORS_FOR_GEARY-KHAMIS_PARITIES_AND_INTERNATIONAL_PRICES/links/54b647560cf28ebe92e7c3d2.pdf.

Rich, Jason T, J. Gail Neely, Randall Paniello, Courtney Voelker, Brian Nussenbaum, and Eric W. Wang. 2010. "A Practical Guide to Understanding Kaplan-Meier Curves." *Otolaryngology -- Head and Neck Surgery* 143: 331–336.

Richards, Peter. 2006. "Death Penalty-Caribbean: When Is It Appropriate to Execute?" Accessed on March 31, 2016. http://www.ipsnews.net/2006/11/death-penalty-caribbean-when-is-it-appropriate-to-execute/.

Roberts-Wray, Kenneth. 1966. *Commonwealth and Colonial Law.* London: Stevens & Sons.

Rokkan, Stein. 1996. "Norway: Numerical Democracy and Corporate Pluralism." In *Political Oppositions in Western Democracies*, edited by R.A. Dahl, 70–115. New Haven: Yale University Press.

Rolle, Domiek. 2012. "Abolish The Privy Council, Easier Said than Done." Accessed on June 16, 2015. http://www.ilntoday.com/files/2012/06/Abolish-The-Privy-Council-by-D-Rolle.pdf.

Romano, Cesare P.R. 2013. "Trial and Error in International Judicialization." In *The Oxford Handbook of International Adjudication*, edited by Cesare P.R. Romano, Karen J. Alter, and Yuval Shany. Oxford: Oxford University Press.

Rosenberg, Gerald N. 2008. *Hollow Hope: Can Courts Bring about Social Change?* Chicago: University of Chicago Press.

Saunders, Adrian. 2010. "The Relevance of the Privy Council in Post Independent West Indian Nation States: 2nd Annual Eugene Dupuch Distinguished Lecture." *Council of Legal Education.* Accessed on February 21, 2016. http://da-academy.org/relevance_privycouncil.pdf.

Scheingold, Stuart, A. 2004. *The Politics of Rights: Lawyers, Public Policy, and Political Change.* Ann Arbor: University of Michigan Press.

Schlesinger, Arthur Meier. 1913. "Colonial Appeals to the Privy Council." *Political Science Quarterly* 28: 433–450.

Schmidt, Peter, and Ann Dryden Witte. 1989. "Predicting Criminal Recidivism using Split Population' Survival Time Models." *Journal of Econometrics* 40, no. 1: 141–159.

Senghore, Aboubacar Abdullah. 2010. "The Judiciary in Governance in The Gambia: The Quest for Autonomy under the Second Republic." *Journal of Third World Studies* 27, no. 2: 215–248.

Seow, Francis T. 1997. "The Politics of Judicial Institutions in Singapore." Accessed on October 19, 2015. http://www.singapore-window.org/1028judi.htm.

Shapiro, Martin. 1981. *Courts: A Comparative and Political Analysis.* Chicago: University of Chicago Press.

Sharples, Jennifer. 2003. "The Legacy of the British Empire," *The Daily Telegraph,* November 3, 2003. http://www.telegraph.co.uk/expat/4190628/Legacy-of-the-British-empire.html.

Slaughter, Anne-Marie. 2000. “Judicial Globalization.” *Virginia Journal of International Law* 40: 1103–1120.

Smith, Joseph Henry. 1950. *Appeals to The Privy Council from The American Plantations*. New York: Columbia University Press.

Stafford, Frank, and George Wheeler. 1901. *The Practice of The Privy Council in Judicial Matters*. London: Sweet and Maxwell, Limited.

Steigerwalt, Amy. 2010. *Battle over the Bench: Senators, Interest Groups and Lower Court Confirmations*. Charlottesville: University of Virginia Press.

Stein, Burton. 2001. *A History of India*. New Delhi and Oxford: Oxford University Press.

Stone Sweet, Alec. 2000. *Governing with Judges: Constitutional Politics in Europe*. Oxford: Oxford University Press.

Straum, Albert L. 1977. “The Procedure of State Constitutional Change—With Special Emphasis on the South and Florida.” *Florida State University Law Review* 5: 569–602.

Streeck, Wolfgang, and Kathleen Thelen. 2005. “Introduction: Institutional Change in Advanced Political Economies.” In *Beyond Continuity—Institutional Change in Advanced Political Economies*, edited by Wolfgang Streeck and Kathleen Thelen, 1–39. Oxford: Oxford University Press.

Strydom, T.J. 2015. “South Africa Plans to Leave the International Criminal Court.” *Reuters*, October 15, 2015. http://www.reuters.com/article/2015/10/11/us-safrica-icc-idUSKCN0S50HM20151011.

Swinfen, David B. 1987. *Imperial Appeal: The Debate on the Appeal to the Privy Council 1833-1986*. Manchester: Manchester University Press.

Tan, Kevin Y.L. 2015. *The Constitution of Singapore: A Conceptual Analysis*. London: Bloomsbury.

Tate, C. Neal, and Stacia L. Haynie. 1993. “Authoritarianism and the Functions of Courts: A Time Series Analysis of the Philippine Supreme Court, 1961-1987.” *Law & Society Review* 27, no. 4: 707–740.

Taylor, Mathew W. 2005. *Judging Policy: Courts and Policy Reform in Democratic Brazil*. Stanford: Stanford University Press.

The Commonwealth. 2015. *Member Countries*. Accessed on March 14, 2017. http://thecommonwealth.org/member-countries.

The High Road to the Caribbean Community. 2017. “The Integrationist Caribbean.” Accessed on June 17, 2019. http://www.theintegrationistcaribbean.org/feature/the-high-road-to-the-caribbean-community/.

The Maddison-Project. 2013. “New Maddison Project Database.” Accessed on June 16, 2015. http://www.ggdc.net/maddison/maddison-project/data.htm.

The National Archives. n.d. “The Judicial Committee Act 1844.” Accessed on March 12, 2017. http://www.legislation.gov.uk/ukpga/Vict/7-8/69/section/1.

The National Archives. n.d. *The Appellate Jurisdiction Act 1876*. Accessed on March 12, 2017. http://www.legislation.gov.uk/ukpga/Vict/39-40/59/contents.

The World Bank. 2017. “World Bank National Accounts Data, and OECD National Accounts Data Files.” Accessed on June 23, 2017. https://data.worldbank.org/indicator/NY.GDP.MKTP.CD.

Toote, Michael D. 2013. *Capital Punishment in The Bahamas: The Privy Council Moratorium*. Bloomington: Author House.

Tran, Mark. 2006. "Fiji's History of Coups." *The Guardian*, December 5, 2006. http://www.theguardian.com/world/2006/dec/05/fiji.travel1.

Travis, Alan, and Nicholas Watt. 2012. "Abu Qatada Deportation Blocked in Human Rights Court." *The Guardian,* January 17, 2012. http://www.theguardian.com/world/2012/jan/17/abu-qatada-deportation-blocked-european.

Travis, Alan. 2015. "Human Rights Act Abolition Will be no "Quick Win" for the Tories." *The Guardian*, May 15, 2015. http://www.theguardian.com/law/2015/may/15/human-rights-act-abolition-will-not-be-quick-win-for-tories.

Tushnet, Mark. 2006. "Political Power and Judicial Power: Some Observations on Their Relationship." *Fordham Law Review* 75, no. 2: 755–768.

University of Illinois Library. 2018. "Stata: Data Analysis and Statistical Software: Getting Started with Stata." Accessed on June 13, 2019. http://guides.library.illinois.edu/STATA.

Veracini, Lorenzo. 2013. "Settler Colonialism: Career of a Concept." *The Journal of Imperial and Commonwealth History* 13, no. 2: 313–333.

Vergne, Jean-Philippe, and Rodolphe Durand. 2010. "The Missing Link between the Theory and Empirics of Path Dependence: Conceptual Clarification, Testability Issue, and Methodological Implications." *Journal of Management Studies* 47, no. 4: 736–760.

Vervaele, John A.E. 2005. "Mercosur and Regional Integration in South America." *International and Comparative Law Quarterly* 54, no. 2: 387–410.

Voigt, Stephan, and Eli M. Salzberger. 2002. "Choosing Not to Choose: When Politicians Choose to Delegate Powers." *Kyklos* 55, no. 2: 247–268.

Voigt, Stephan, Michael Ebeling, and Lorenz Blume. 2007. "Improving Credibility by Delegating Judicial Competence-the Case of the Judicial Committee of the Privy Council." *Journal of Development Economics* 82, no. 2: 348–393.

Watt, Nicholas. 2015. "Cameron Refuses to Rule out leaving the European Convention on Human Rights." *The Guardian*, June 3, 2015. http://www.theguardian.com/law/2015/jun/03/cameron-refuses-to-rule-out-leavingeuropean-convention-on-human-rights.

Watts, Carl P. 2010. "British Decolonization.' In *World History Encyclopedia Era 9: Promises and Paradoxes1945-Present, Parts I and II*, edited by Fred Nadis and Jack Waskey. Santa Barbara: ABC-CLIO.

Whittington, Keith. 2007. *The Political Foundations of Judicial Supremacy: The Presidency, the Supreme Court, and Constitutional Leadership in U.S. History.* Princeton: Princeton University Press.

Wiles, Stephen. 2014. "International Courts and Tribunals." *Harvard Law School Library*. http://guides.library.harvard.edu/content.php?pid=100079&sid=757052.

Williams, Richard. 2015. "Interaction Effects between Continuous Variables (Optional)." Accessed on May 3, 2016. https://www3.nd.edu/~rwilliam/stats2/l55.pdf.

Wilson, Margaret. 2000. "Discussion Paper: Reshaping New Zealand's Appeal Structure." Office of the Attorney-General, Parliament Buildings: Wellington, New

Zealand. Accessed on December 14, 2015. http://www.crownlaw.govt.nz/uploads/PCDiscuss.pdf.

Wilson, Margaret. 2000. "Reshaping New Zealand's Appeal Structure Discussion Paper 4/4." Accessed on January 29, 2016. https://www.beehive.govt.nz/feature/reshaping-new-zealands-appeal-structure-discussion-paper-44.

Wilson, Margaret. 2010. "From Privy Council to Supreme: A Rite of Passage for New Zealand's Legal System." Accessed on February 18, 2016. https://researchcommons.waikato.ac.nz/bitstream/handle/10289/5686/The%20Harkness%20Henry%20Lecture.pdf?sequence=1&isAllowed=y.

Wilson, Margaret. 2010. "Who Makes the Law? The Role of the Supreme Court in New Zealand's Constitutional Arrangements." Accessed on December 14, 2015. http://www.nzuklinkfoundation.org/uploads/files/20101101_Who_Makes_the_Law_Lectu re_Final_Script_(2).pdf.

World Trade Organization. 2015. "Understanding the World Trade Organization: The Organization." Accessed on October 3, 2015. https://www.wto.org/english/thewto_e/whatis_e/tif_e/org2_e.htm.

Yakana, David. 2006. "Employers and Labour-Management Relations: The Guyana Experience in Industrial Relations in the Caribbean Issues and Perspectives." Accessed on October 3, 2015. http://www.ilo.org/wcmsp5/groups/public/---americas/---ro-lima/---sro-port_of_spain/documents/publication/wcms_224310.pdf.

Yusuf, Hakeem O. 2014. *Colonial and Post-Colonial Constitutionalism in the Commonwealth: Peace, Order and Good Government*. Abingdon: Routledge.

Zorn, Jean G. 1994. "Custom Then and Now: The Changing Melanesian Family." In *Custom and Customary Law: Coursebook Two*, 95–123. USP: Suva.

Index

Note: Page numbers followed by "n" refer to notes.

About the Author

Harold A. Young is an Assistant Professor at Austin Peay State University (APSU) in Clarksville, Tennessee. He has a PhD in Philosophy (Political Science) from Georgia State University (GSU) and JD (LLB/CLE) from the University of the West Indies/Norman Manley School of Law. He is a member of the Belize Bar where he practiced law before immigrating to the United States. Dr. Young's research interests include the death penalty, American and international perspectives on judicial institutional changes, and decision-making. His law practice sparked an interest in judicial institutions generally and, more specifically, the Judicial Committee of the Privy Council on which much of his research is based. His current project, "The Survival of Gangs: Institution or Outlaw?" involves extensive fieldwork in his native Belize. He currently serves as the Chair of the APSU Institution Review Board, member of the Survey Policy and Oversight Committee, a director of The Woodward Library Society, the faculty advisor to the Pre-Law Society, the Campus NAACP, and a cadre of political science students. As a director of the All Saint's Alumni Foundation, he raises funds to send deserving students to high school in Belize.

Dr. Young is the recipient of a Top Blogger Recognition from Midwest Political Science Association, John A. Garcia Scholarship to the Inter-University Consortium for Political and Social Research, Glenn Abney Fellowship for most promising Public Law student (GSU), and a Price Fellowship (Centers for Disease Control). His work is published in the *Journal of Race, Politics & International Social Studies Review*, *Endarch: Journal of Black Political Research*, *Journal of International & Global Studies*, and the *Journal of Global South Studies*.

www.ingramcontent.com/pod-product-compliance
Ingram Content Group UK Ltd.
Pitfield, Milton Keynes, MK11 3LW, UK
UKHW012119150926
475560UK00002B/182

9 781498 586948